Constance Hill

Story of the Princess des Ursins in Spain

Constance Hill

Story of the Princess des Ursins in Spain

ISBN/EAN: 9783337167196

Printed in Europe, USA, Canada, Australia, Japan

Cover: Foto ©ninafisch / pixelio.de

More available books at **www.hansebooks.com**

STORY OF THE
PRINCESS DES URSINS
IN SPAIN
(CAMARERA-MAYOR)

BY

CONSTANCE HILL
EDITOR OF "FREDERIC HILL" ETC.

"Elle régna en Espagne, et son histoire mériterait d'être écrite"
ST. SIMON

With Twelve Portraits and a Frontispiece

LONDON
WILLIAM HEINEMANN
1899

THIS BOOK IS

Dedicated to

TWO PARIS FRIENDS

ONE OF THE PAST

AND

ONE OF THE PRESENT

JOHN DIGWEED AND
JULES TRAYER

PREFACE

We sometimes meet with a character in old French memoirs which seems so completely to live for us that, in spite of its antique surroundings, it steps on to the stage of our very existence and claims an interest as for a friend of to-day. Thus it was with the present writer and the Princess des Ursins. Meeting her for the first time, some years ago, in the volumes of St. Simon, an interest of this kind was created which went on increasing as fresh sources of contemporary information were discovered to throw new light on her strong personality and on her strangely eventful career.

The Princess des Ursins was a central and dominant figure in Spain during the turmoil and chaos of the Wars of the Spanish Succession.

Forced by circumstances to come to the front, she reigned for twelve years "behind the flimsy veil of a phantom king," with a power that was almost absolute. Her political career has been harshly judged in England, where her character and motives are little known, but she has received better treatment in France. This, perhaps, is natural, since she was a French woman and was an upholder of the Bourbon dynasty in Spain, while, on the other hand, she was looked upon by the English as an enemy. But time has broken down the barriers between her friends and her foes of nearly two hundred years ago, and we can now judge the conduct of the Princess with impartiality. Her letters are before us—letters written to intimate friends with openness and sincerity and with a charm of style peculiar to a lively and talented French woman of the early eighteenth century.

These intimate friends were Madame de Maintenon and the Maréchale de Noailles. To them the writer could express her thoughts and opinions without reserve and without fear of misconstruction, and could give free scope to her bright nature that was ever ready to see the hopeful and even humorous side of affairs, however gloomy they might appear to others. "Mon Dieu, Madame!" exclaims Madame de Maintenon, "how happy you are! and how delightfully you jest! There is never a tinge of bitterness in what you say. Your gaiety of heart finds its way even to my heart, and gives me the only cheerfulness I can boast of at present." And again she writes: "You have a good courage, a happy vein of humour, and a hopeful temperament; these are powerful aids in overcoming misfortune."

Madame des Ursins' letters are written under a variety of circumstances, and while, at times, they are playful in tone, at others they are deeply in earnest. Sometimes it is the champion of the young King and Queen who speaks, and we find her, when occasion requires, boldly opposing the "Grand Monarque" himself. Sometimes it is the keen politician contending with Torcy and Chamillart; at others it is the organiser of armies. Sometimes, again, it is the woman who has been injured, but who is calm and dignified in defeat; at others it is the woman laden with honours who is equally calm and dignified in her triumph.

Madame des Ursins was ambitious in the right sense of the word. She desired to have free scope for gifts of mind and character that she could not but be conscious of possessing. Still she took up politics mainly from the woman's point of view—that of the affections. Her attachment to the young Queen Marie-Louise of Savoy was her strongest incentive to action. In one of her letters to Madame de Maintenon, she remarks: "It is a high honour, no doubt, to live in close connection with the great ones of the world, but the honour is dearly bought when those great ones are loved as we love them, so that our thoughts are completely absorbed in their concerns, making us totally forget our own."

In the same way Madame des Ursins, when working for Spain, could forget that she was a French woman. On one occasion, when the Grandees were opposing her measures as those of a foreigner, an Irish Colonel in the Spanish service, named Burke, remarked: "Leave her alone, and you will find when the interests of Spain are attacked she will be a truer Spaniard than any of you." A prophecy which was amply fulfilled.

The first letters of the Princess des Ursins that were published appeared in 1777. They consist of a small selection that were introduced into the "Mémoires de Noailles"—a book which has furnished many curious details connected with the lady's career in Spain. In 1806 a series of her letters appeared, forming one small volume, addressed for the most part to Marshal Villeroy, and edited by Mons. L. Collin. In 1826 the entire correspondence of herself and Madame de Maintenon, which fills four volumes octavo, was published by Bossange Frères. The original documents of this correspondence had passed into the possession of Louis XV. As the letters threw light on many State affairs, the King allowed his chief Minister, the Duc de Choiseul, to make a copy of them, and it was from a descendant of this same Duke that the MS. was obtained by Bossange.

In 1859 a fresh series of letters of the Princess was given to the public by Mons. A. Geffroy, who had discovered them, strangely enough, among the archives in the Royal Library at Stockholm. They were not the original documents, but careful copies. How they found their way to Stockholm Mons. Geffroy is unable to say, but he suggests that they were among the numberless family documents that were scattered far and wide at the time of the French Revolution. Mons. Geffroy has preceded the letters by an interesting biographical sketch of the Princess.

About the same time that this work was published, another work upon the Princess des Ursins appeared, being a critical "Review of her Life and Character as a Politician," by François Combes. In this "Review," which forms a large and closely printed volume, every event in her career is commented upon, and her claims to the esteem of posterity weighed in the balance. Ste. Beuve remarks : "In this process of careful revision and criticism, Madame des Ursins' reputation has by no means suffered, it has gained by the light thrown upon it." And referring to her letters, of which more than four hundred are now made public, another critic remarks, "that even in the ease of unrestraint, she never abandoned a pure and lofty style of diction. It is the special honour," he adds, "of the epoch to which she belonged to give us in the documents which furnish its history models of sound literature and of good taste."

CONSTANCE HILL.

GROVE COTTAGE, FROGNAL,
HAMPSTEAD.
November 1898.

CONTENTS

CHAP.		PAGE
I.	A Vacant Throne	1
II.	A Child-Queen and Her Guide	12
III.	The Evil Genius of Spain	27
IV.	Clouds Gather and the Storm Bursts	43
V.	Fortune's Changes	65
VI.	A Spanish Ovation	81
VII.	A Royal Fugitive	104
VIII.	A New Hope	126
IX.	Tidings of Victory	139
X.	Joy in the Palace	150
XI.	Reverses	162
XII.	Left to Fight Alone	176
XIII.	Treachery in the Camp	187
XIV.	A Cause Won	200
XV.	A Wily Priest	208
XVI.	A King's Gratitude	221
XVII.	Peace after Storm	232

LIST OF ILLUSTRATIONS

"*Happy occasion of the birth of the Prince of Asturias, August 25, 1707,*" *with portrait of the Princess des Ursins on the left. Below are depicted scenes of national rejoicing, including M. Amelot's* "*Fountain of Wine.*" *Victory of Almanza in the centre.* . *Frontispiece*

Louis XIV. in old age, by Rigaud .	To face page	4
Philip V., King of Spain .	,,	14
Marie Louise of Savoy, Queen of Spain	,,	20
Cardinal Portocarero	,,	30
Cardinal d'Estrée .	,,	44
Duc de St. Simon, by de Troy .	,,	62
The Pretender, styled "Jacques III., Roi d'Angleterre, agé de 16 ans," by de Troy .	,,	72
The Archduke Charles represented as Charles III. of Spain. Inscribed "Carolus III. D.G., Hispaniorum et Indiarum Rex" . .	,,	92

LIST OF ILLUSTRATIONS

Doorway of the House of the Cordón, Burgos	To face page	114
Duke of Berwick, Generalissimo of the Forces in Spain	,,	142
Duke of Orleans (afterwards Regent of France), by de Troy	,,	184
Louis Joseph, duc de Vendôme	,,	206

WORKS CONSULTED

"Princesse des Ursins. Lettres inédites à M. le Maréchal de Villeroy, suivies de sa correspondance avec Madame de Maintenon." L. Collin, Paris. 1806.

Lettres inédites de Mme. de Maintenon et de Mme. la Princesse des Ursins. Bossange Frères, Paris. 1826.

Lettres inédites de la Princesse des Ursins, avec une introduction et des notes. Par M. A. Geffroy. Paris. 1859.

"La Princesse des Ursins. Essai sur sa vie et son caractère politique." Par M. François Combes. Paris. 1858.

"Mémoires du Duc de Noailles." M. l'Abbé Millot. Maestricht. 1777.

"Mémoires du Marquis de San Phélipe, pour servir à l'histoire d'Espagne sous le regne de Philippe V." Traduits par le Chevalier de Maudave. Amsterdam. 1756.

"Mémoires du Duc de Saint-Simon." Paris. 1829.

"Avènement des Bourbons au trône d'Espagne." Par Henri, Duc d'Harcourt, avec des notes par C. Hippeau. Paris. 1875.

"Mémoires secrets du Marquis de Louville." Paris. 1818.

"Mémoires du Maréchal de Berwick," écrits par lui-même. Paris. 1778.

WORKS CONSULTED

"Mémoires secrets de Duclos." 1791.

"La Cour et la ville de Madrid vers le fin du 17ᵉ siècle." Par Me. la Comtesse d'Aulnoy. Me. Carey (éditeur).

"Lettres de Madame de Villars à Madame de Coulanges." A. de Courtois (éditeur). Paris. 1868.

"Lettres intimes de J. M. Alberoni, adressées au Comte I. Rocca," avec des notes par Emile Bourgeois. Paris. 1893.

"Causeries du Lundi." Par C.-A. Sainte-Beuve. Paris.

"History of the War of the Succession in Spain." By Lord Mahon. London. 1832.

"Kings of Spain of the House of Bourbon." By Archdeacon Coxe. London. 1815.

"History of England." By Lord Macaulay. London. 1861.

"Critical and Historical Essays." By Lord Macaulay. London. Ed. 1874.

"A History of France." By G. W. Kitchin, D.D. Oxford. 1885.

"French Women of Letters." By Julia Kavanagh. London. 1862.

"Elizabeth Farnese." By Edward Armstrong, M.A. London. 1892.

CHAPTER I

A VACANT THRONE

A CURIOUS scene was enacted in the palace of Madrid on the 1st of November in the year 1700, which is described in the Memoirs of St. Simon. Charles II., the weak, imbecile King of Spain, had just died. He was childless, and no one knew who would be proclaimed by his will to be his successor. For long past the royal families of France and Austria, equally related to the King, had been intriguing to secure the prize. "No sooner had the King expired," writes St. Simon, "than the opening of the will had to take place. An event so strange, of such vast importance, and which would affect the interests of so many millions of people, attracted all Madrid to the palace; so that the rooms adjoining the Council-chamber where the will was being read were crowded almost to suffocation. The foreign ambassadors were conspicious as they pushed eagerly forward, each anxious to be the first to inform his Court of the choice made by the King. Blécourt (French chargé d'affaires) was there, like the rest, for he was as ignorant respecting the secret as they were. The Count d'Harrach, the Emperor's Ambassador, was standing just in front of the door of the Council-chamber. He bore himself triumphantly, for he relied upon the will's being made in favour of the Archduke, and his hopes for his own future were high. At last the door opened for a moment and the Duke d'Abrantés appeared, a man much feared for his malicious wit. He had slipped out of the Council-chamber as soon as the reading of the will was over for the enjoyment of disclosing the great secret. He was instantly beset by the crowd. He gazed calmly upon them but maintained a solemn silence. Blécourt approached. The Duke regarded him vacantly, and then turning away his head, appeared to be searching for some other person. This action surprised Blécourt and was interpreted by all as auguring ill for France. Suddenly the Duke seemed to become aware of the presence of the Count d'Harrach. An expression of joy illumined his countenance, and, throwing himself into his arms, he exclaimed aloud in Spanish, 'Señor, it is with great pleasure'—here he made a pause and again embraced him—'Yes, Señor, it is with heartfelt joy that from henceforth'—here he made a second pause. 'It is indeed with infinite satisfaction that I now part from you and take a final leave of the august House of Austria!' The astonishment and indignation of the Count d'Harrach took from him all power of utterance. . . . He stood quite still for a moment, and then quitted the room, fuming with rage and disappointment."

The will decreed the successor to the vast dominions of the Spanish crown "on which the sun never set" to be the young Duke of Anjou, grandson of Louis XIV., and soon afterwards he was proclaimed King, as the reader will remember, under the title of Philip V. On the 4th of December following, the young man, who was but seventeen years of age, quitted the French Court to take possession of his kingdom. Louis XIV. bade him farewell in his own dramatic style. " Go, my son," he exclaimed, embracing him, " go: the Pyrenees exist no longer!"

The "Grand Monarque," who ruled his own family as despotically as he ruled his people, soon made choice of a wife for his grandson. The Princess he fixed upon was Marie Louise of Savoy, a daughter of the Duke of Savoy and a younger sister of the Duchess of Burgundy. Marie Louise was only thirteen years of age, and it was, therefore, necessary to provide her with a female companion, who could give her help and guidance in her new and exalted position. Such help and guidance could only be given by a lady holding a high official post which would entitle her to live in close connection with the royal couple. Fortunately such a post already existed in the Court of Spain—that of Camarera-Mayor or

LOUIS XIV (IN OLD AGE)

Superintendent of the Queen's Household—and that it should be ably filled became a matter of first importance.

Louis XIV. wrote to the Duc d'Harcourt, French Ambassador at Madrid (July 7th, 1701):* "As the King of Spain is of a gentle, yielding disposition, it will be an easy matter for the Queen to acquire a powerful influence over his mind. Nothing can be known as yet of the disposition of the Princess of Savoy. She is of too tender an age to entertain thoughts of ruling at present, but that same tender age is keenly susceptible to all kinds of impressions." Louis enlarges upon the dangers of placing persons of doubtful character or intentions in close proximity to the Queen. He then informs his Ambassador that after due consideration he has decided that the high post of Camarera-Mayor can be confided to no one with so much propriety as to the Princess des Ursins. "Her late husband the Duc de Bracciano," he remarks, "head of the House of Orsini, was a grandee of Spain.

* "Mémoires et Correspondance du Duc d'Harcourt."

She has passed much of her life in foreign countries; she knows the ways and customs of Spain; and together with these advantages she possesses an alert and powerful mind and much urbanity of demeanour, so that she is especially qualified to instruct a young Princess in the art of ruling a Court with dignity."

Who then was this Princess des Ursins to whom so important a post was to be confided? At the time that Louis XIV.'s letter was written the Princess was the central figure of a brilliant society in Rome. The Duc de Bracciano and Prince Orsini, for he bore both titles, was an Italian nobleman of high rank and political influence, and at the Orsini Palace were to be seen all the illustrious people who met together in the Holy City. The Princess des Ursins (for her name was afterwards rendered in French), was a person of consequence in the eyes of the French Court, for she had done much to further French interests in Rome, and was enjoying a pension from Louis XIV. in recognition of her services.

The Princess des Ursins belonged to the

family of La Trimouille, and therefore to the French nobility, on her father's side; on her mother's to the legal and commercial classes, whence perhaps she derived her sagacity. She was born not later than 1642, but the exact date is not known. Her first husband was a Prince de Chalais, and the young Princess de Chalais "shone at the Hotel d'Albret by the side of Madame de Sevigné." But the Prince had to fly from France on account of being concerned in a fatal duel. He took refuge in Spain, where he and his wife passed several years, and where the lady formed friendships that were to prove invaluable in the future. Soon after quitting Spain the Prince de Chalais died, and his widow took up her residence in Rome. Here it was that some years later she married the Prince Orsini.

After this second marriage the lady occasionally paid visits to Paris, and it was during these visits that she became acquainted with the Duke de St. Simon. The Princess plays a conspicuous part in his Memoirs. The following description of her, which we have somewhat condensed, occurs in the third volume:

"She was rather tall—a brunette, but with blue eyes, which gave expression to every varying sentiment she wished to convey. Her figure was perfect. She had a beautiful throat; and her face, though not strictly handsome, was charming. Her air was extremely noble, and there was something even majestic in her bearing, yet at the same time there was ease and grace in every turn or gesture. Her voice was melodious and her intonation extremely agreeable. Her manners were flattering and engaging, and their charm, when she chose to exert it, irresistible. I have never," he continues, "met her equal whether in personal or in intellectual gifts. Madame des Ursins' conversation was brilliant, and it seemed to flow from an inexhaustible source; yet no word or gesture escaped her to express that which she wished to conceal. A natural gaiety of disposition was, in her case, combined with ready tact and sound judgment, and with an equability of temper which left her, at all times and under all circumstances, complete mistress of herself. She was ambitious, but hers was an exalted

AN UNACKNOWLEDGED QUEEN

ambition soaring above the usual aspirations of her sex or the common ambition of men."

During her visits to Paris the Princess des Ursins formed the friendship of Madame de Maintenon, and in later years the two ladies carried on a regular correspondence. This correspondence, which was strictly confidential, brings into bold relief the widely differing characteristics of each.

Madame de Maintenon, that "unacknowledged Queen of France," who was by nature reserved and grave, and who shunned the noise and bustle of society, delighted in the energy, hopefulness, and humour which characterised the Princess's letters. On one occasion, after lamenting the coarse manners of some of the ladies at Versailles, she writes: "For my part I love those women who are modest, sober, cheerful; able alike to be serious or to be merry, *railleuses d'une raillerie qui enferme une louange*, whose heart is right, and whose conversation is lively and inspiring." This description, which was evidently intended for a portrait of her friend, was no flattery. Madame des

Ursins possessed to the full what Voltaire has termed "le grand art de plaire."

The Prince Orsini died before the beginning of the eighteenth century, but the Princess continued to live in Rome. Being, however, well informed of all that went on at Versailles, she had early intelligence that the appointment of a Camarera-Mayor to the new Queen of Spain was under debate, and she saw clearly that, could she obtain the post, a wide field for the exercise of all her special talents would lie before her. To many it would seem strange that the Princess des Ursins, at the age of fifty-nine years, should desire to give up her assured position in Rome for a new and untried career in a foreign land. A French lady (Madame de Coulanges) expressed, we are told, much surprise on hearing that she coveted this appointment, for this lady imagined that to a person of the Princess's age life could offer nothing that was new and attractive. "Her view of the case," remarks a great French critic, "proves that Madame de Coulanges was merely a woman, and was unable to comprehend the influence upon her own sex of any passions save those of the affections. But Madame des Ursins was born to mould and direct great public affairs and to have a high hand in the intrigues of States."

CHAPTER II

A CHILD-QUEEN AND HER GUIDE

IN September, 1701, Philip V. and Marie Louise of Savoy were married by proxy at Turin, and Madame des Ursins received instructions to repair to Lombardy in order to meet her royal mistress and conduct her into Spain. The meeting took place at Villafranca, a small town on the coast of Lombardy.

Madame des Ursins was pleased, from the first, with the young Queen; and her own bright nature and ready tact, her long acquaintance with Italian life, and her knowledge of the country to which they were bound, all made her presence valuable as well as attractive to Marie Louise. The importance of such a companion was especially felt when they reached the frontiers of Spain; where the

Queen was met by the ladies-in-waiting of the Spanish Court, and where, to her surprise and sorrow, all her friends and attendants of the Ducal Court of Savoy were at once dismissed.

The royal marriage was to be re-celebrated at Figueras, a border town of Catalonia, whither Philip V. repaired to receive his bride. A pretty account is given of their first meeting, which recalls to the mind of the reader the tale of " Lalla Rookh."

Finding on his arrival at Figueras that Marie Louise was still some distance from that place, Philip determined to go forward to meet her. But since the rigid etiquette of Spain forbade the King's crossing the border, he travelled incognito accompanied by very few attendants. On approaching the village of Hostelnuovo he beheld the bridal train slowly advancing and, amidst the gay cavalcade, saw the gilded litter, slung between mules, in which the young Queen and her Camarera-Mayor were seated. Philip dismounted, and running to the litter presented himself as a messenger sent by the King to inquire after the health of the royal traveller. The Queen answered his questions graciously, and herself inquired after the King's health, but beginning to suspect the stratagem, her answers became more and more friendly, till at last she proposed to alight in order that they might converse more at their ease. The King put out his hand to protest against this, and the bride, now fully convinced of the identity of her lover, took the royal hand between both of hers and kissed it. The King dared not assume his real character, but he returned, well satisfied, to Figueras.

After the wedding festivities were concluded the royal couple continued their journey. Madame des Ursins writes, *en route*, to her friend, the wife of Marshal Noailles, " Bon Dieu! Madame, what a queer employment you have all found for me! I have not a moment's leisure, not even time to speak to my secretary. I cannot rest after dinner nor eat when I am hungry. I think myself happy if I can snatch a mouthful in the midst of business, for I rarely sit down to table without being called away. Madame de Maintenon would

PHILIP V., KING OF SPAIN

laugh if she knew the particulars of my responsibilities. Pray tell her that it is I alone who am privileged to take the King of Spain's dressing-gown from him when he gets into bed, and to present it to him with his slippers when he rises. So far I do all with patience, but it is really ludicrous that each night, when the King enters the Queen's chamber, the Count de Benevente presents *me* with His Majesty's sword and with a lamp whose oil I usually upset over my clothes. The King would never rise if I did not draw aside the curtains of his bed, for it would be considered sacrilege for any one but myself to enter the chamber. The other night the lamp went out because I had spilt half the oil. In the morning I did not know where to find the windows, which I had not seen uncovered, owing to our arrival at the place after dark. I thought I should have broken my nose against the walls, and there were the King of Spain and myself jostling against each other in the dark for nearly a quarter of an hour feeling about for the shutters!"

But very different duties and responsibilities were soon to fall to the share of the Princess des Ursins. Not only the internal management of a royal household but the external government of a great State was to depend largely upon her guiding—a State, moreover, where the chains of custom took the place of law, and superstition the place of religion.

The Reformation had never penetrated into Spain. "While other nations," writes Macaulay, "were putting away childish things the Spaniard still thought as a child and understood as a child. Among the men of the seventeenth century he was the man of the fifteenth century or of a still darker period, delighted to behold an *auto-da-fé* and ready to volunteer on a crusade. . . . The evils produced by a bad government and a bad religion seemed to have attained their greatest height during the last years of the seventeenth century. . . . An undisciplined army, a rotting fleet, an empty treasury were all that remained of that which had been so great."

The domestic life of a country in such a

condition could not but be constrained and gloomy. The laws and customs affecting women were strongly Oriental in their cast, having their origin in the days of the Moorish rule. Women of the upper classes lived for the most part in seclusion apart from men. Even when they drove out it was in coaches *lourds comme des maisons*, behind curtains closely drawn. The windows of their apartments were also carefully screened from public view. A French lady writing from Madrid towards the end of the seventeenth century remarks : " This city has the appearance of one vast closely barred cage. All the windows and balconies from ground to roof have outside shutters, and we catch glimpses through their narrow openings of poor ladies peeping at the passers-by." In the royal palace of Madrid some of the rooms occupied by the ladies of the Court had actually no windows whatever, and received their only light from apertures in the doors. In these dimly lighted rooms the ladies lived a life of idleness and dull monotony such as may still be seen in Eastern harems. It is true their apartments were decorated with Eastern magnificence. All the kingdoms ruled by Spain contributed their stores of wealth and art to adorn her palaces. The gathering together of their treasures recalls the days of Solomon. Naples and Sicily provided pictures, Sardinia and Milan statues and delicate embroideries, the Netherlands sent tapestries, and the far-off Indies gold, silver, and jewels. But splendour is a poor exchange for liberty.

The position of a Queen of Spain was even worse than that of her ladies-in-waiting, for she was hemmed in by specially stringent rules of etiquette whose antiquity rendered them sacred in the eyes of the Spaniards. Madame de Villars, wife of the French Ambassador at Charles II.'s Court, who visited Madrid twenty years earlier than the accession of Philip V., thus writes: "The tedium of existence in the palace is almost crushing. I sometimes remark to our Princess,* on entering her chamber, that one seems to feel it, to see it, to touch it, so

---

* A daughter of the Duke of Orleans recently married to Charles II.

tangible appears the monotonous gloom around us." Court life had not changed since these words were written, and we find Madame des Ursins thus describing the society of the palace : " The Court ladies, on entering the royal apartments, kneel to kiss the Queen's hand, and then silently seat themselves upon the ground at her feet. If her Majesty and I did not keep up some sort of conversation it would cease altogether. We ask our guests if they are fond of dancing, if they sing or play upon any musical instrument, if they are fond of walking, or if they play at cards ? To all these questions they answer 'no.'"

We seem to see the group of silent ladies in their stiff Spanish costumes seated cross-legged upon the ground, and the young Queen and her friend vainly endeavouring to make them talk ! The Court dress of that day resembled armour rather than clothing. Its wearer's shoulders were so compressed as to render it impossible to raise the arms ; the bosom was flattened by heavy weights and the body encased in long stiff stays. There is a portrait of Marie Louise of Savoy at the British Museum, taken soon after her marriage, which represents her wearing Spanish attire. The round childish face and tender throat emerge pathetically from their rigid framework.

The Court jewelry consisted chiefly of heavy ecclesiastical ornaments. Images of saints were fastened to the ladies' bodices or sleeves, and they wore belts formed of cases containing relics. They carried rosaries in their hands which they were continually counting. "Such customs," writes Madame des Ursins, "may have their merit, but they are not calculated to inspire cheerfulness."

Madame des Ursins exerted herself to enliven this dismal Court. She inaugurated concerts where she delighted to produce the Italian music then just coming into vogue. She even ventured to introduce dancing as a Court pastime, and persuaded the King and Queen to occasionally lead off the dance. This last was a bold innovation, for hitherto the Queens of Spain had been jealously kept out of sight and had not been permitted to mingle with the

MARIE LOUISE OF SAVOY, QUEEN OF SPAIN

ordinary life of their Court. She introduced dramatic entertainments where Molière's wit was heard for the first time. What a contrast his plays must have formed to the old Spanish dramas! These were long and solemn, and rather resembled a religious service than a comedy. If an actor made a confession or uttered a saint's name the spectators fell on their knees and prayed aloud. Even the social character of the audience was destroyed by a strict separation of the sexes, who sat on either side of a thick curtain hung down the middle of the theatre.

We can easily imagine that in a life so surrounded by artificial restraints there must have been a great craving for excitement. This craving, which Madame des Ursins endeavoured to appease by natural and innocent pleasures, had till now found a vent in the appalling scenes of cruelty perpetrated by the Inquisition. The *autos-da-fé* formed part of the great pageants held in honour of State events, and the Kings and Queens of Spain with their Court formed part of the audience. Philip's predecessor,

Charles II., made a special request to the Grand Inquisitor in the year 1680 that an *auto-da-fé* should be held in Madrid in honour of his recent marriage. There exists a curious contemporary account of the whole proceedings, written by a Spaniard named Joseph del Olmo, which gives a vivid idea of the feeling of the day respecting the terrible institution. Olmo was the architect who designed the great theatre in the Plaza Mayor where the executions took place. In the centre there rose, we are told, an enormous scaffold which was so placed as to be close to the King's palace. Seats in the theatre were apportioned to all the chief dignitaries of the State, and the balconies of the surrounding mansions were filled by the ladies of the Court in their gala dress. An immense concourse of people attended the scene. When all was in readiness the captain of the Inquisition troops entered the royal palace, "bearing," writes Olmo, "a small faggot gracefully ornamented with ribbons meet to be placed before the eyes of majesty. The Duke de Pastrano, having received the faggot from the captain, conveyed it to the King, who at once seized it with his own royal hand and carried it to the Queen that she might gaze upon the precious object. The King then returned the faggot to the Duke, who, in his turn, restored it to the captain with these words: 'His Majesty desires that this faggot shall be the first thrown into the flames, and that it be thrown in his name.'" On arriving at the scene of execution the King, Olmo tells us, took a solemn oath in the presence of the vast multitude assembled to "persecute all heretics and apostates, and ever to aid the Holy Inquisition in the accomplishment of its work, so agreeable to God and so essential to the glory of religion." As the executions proceeded, the spectators roused to a pitch of brutal excitement tortured the unhappy victims before the flames could reach them. Some burnt them with lighted torches, some struck them with their swords, others hurled stones at them. The King, we are told, stood upon his balcony watching this scene of massacre with "unflagging interest and pious enjoyment." Olmo concludes his narrative by extolling his behaviour, and declaring that it was "worthy of the admiration of mankind."*

Madame de Villars, who was at Madrid at the time, wrote to a friend: "I had not the courage to be present at the horrible execution of the Jews. It was an appalling spectacle from what I hear. But, nevertheless, my absence has given much offence, as I was expected to be present and to find *great amusement* in the sight."†

Madame des Ursins, fearless of the results that might accrue to herself, ventured to oppose the all-powerful Inquisition, "the evil genius of Spain." She advised Philip V. to discountenance the *autos-da-fé*, and he declared openly that he would not sanction them with his presence. Scenes of cruelty had no attraction for Philip. His faults were not those of a cruel but of a weak character. When he succeeded to the throne of Spain, his grandfather Louis XIV. wrote thus of him to the Duc

---

* Notes par A. de Courtois sur "Les Lettres de Madame de Villars à Madame de Coulanges."

† The expression in the French is *me divertir tout à fait*.

d'Harcourt, then French Ambassador at Madrid (December 15, 1700): "It is well for me to inform you that the King of Spain's intentions are good. He wishes to do right, and will do it if he understands how. But this understanding is what he lacks. He is not well-informed, less so, indeed, than is usual at his age. It will be an easy task to govern him. . . . He will have confidence in you and will follow your counsels. . . . Be assured that I rely implicitly upon you."

Ill health had obliged the Duc d'Harcourt to quit Spain soon after the new reign commenced. Fortunately for the young King there was again a strong mind at hand whose counsels were wise and just. By the advice of the Princess des Ursins Philip sought to obtain the goodwill of his subjects. He followed their rules of etiquette as far as possible, adopted the Spanish costume, spoke the Spanish language, and was careful to observe their religious rites and ceremonies. The young Queen was guided by her Camarera-Mayor through many a difficulty that attended her first residence at a Court so different from the bright Italian home that she had left, and soon her own engaging manners won the heart of the Spaniards.

Thus the Bourbon dynasty began to take root, while Madame des Ursins, fully aware of the jealousy with which a Frenchwoman high in office was regarded, kept herself as far as possible in the background.

CHAPTER III

THE EVIL GENIUS OF SPAIN

IMPORTANT reforms were gradually and cautiously introduced into the Court. One of these was the reduction of the royal household, which had been very large under the Austrian kings. It was a custom in Spain for both king and nobles to take over, together with their inheritance, all the retinue, including slaves and pensioners, of their predecessor, without dismissing any of their own followers; so that the households, with their dependencies, kept on increasing in numbers. A visitor at the Court of Charles II. writes: "I am told that the King provides daily food in Madrid alone for ten thousand persons." Probably this was no exaggeration, for we learn from the same writer that some of the wives of the richer grandees had as many as five hundred female attendants.

In reducing the King's household an example of economy was set which it was hoped the nobility would follow.

A small reform of a more delicate and personal nature was attempted by the young Queen. Spanish Court etiquette, which perpetuated many a Moorish custom, had decreed that women's feet must never be visible. Even the doors and steps of carriages were so constructed as to conceal them. The ladies for this reason wore a long and cumbersome overskirt called the "tantillo." "The Queen Marie of Savoy," writes the Duc de Noailles, "wished the ladies of the palace to follow her example by discarding the tantillo. This proposed innovation was actually regarded as an affair of State! Some gentlemen went so far as to declare that they would rather see their wives lying dead before them than that their feet should be seen! The Ambassador Blécourt wrote gravely (to his Court) that a descent of the English upon all the coasts of Spain would have caused less commotion." The Queen succeeded, however, in ousting the tantillo, and the Court ladies finally acknowledged that they were relieved from a heavy burden.

The enemies of the Bourbon dynasty had up to this time permitted its peaceable settlement in Spain, but an event now occurred which determined them to uproot it forthwith. James II. died at St. Germains, and Louis XIV. at once recognised his son as King of England and caused him to be proclaimed in France by the title of James III. Up to this time King William had been unable to persuade the English people to go to war with France upon the question of the Spanish succession, but the recognition of the Pretender was "the one thing needed to enlist the whole force of English opinion on his side." "The cry for war," says Macaulay, "was raised by the city of London and echoed and re-echoed from every corner of the realm. . . . Before the commencement of active hostilities William was no more, but the Grand Alliance of the European Powers against the Bourbons was already constructed.

On the 16th May, 1702, war was proclaimed, by concert, at Vienna, at London, and at the Hague." Thus began the long Wars of the Spanish Succession.

There was a large party in Spain in favour of the Archduke Charles, the Austrian claimant to the throne, and all disaffected persons were ready, at the first good opportunity, to join his standard. Even in the Court of Madrid the allegiance of the Spanish grandees to their Bourbon King grew more and more wavering as report after report arrived of the defeats that France was sustaining in the Netherlands and elsewhere.

In the spring of 1702 Philip V. joined the campaign in Italy, hoping by his presence to arouse the enthusiasm of his Neapolitan subjects. During his absence the young Queen was created Regent, and in that capacity she had to attend the sittings of the Junta. Madame des Ursins accompanied her, and was thus enabled to judge for herself of the characters of the men in power. Chief of these was the Cardinal Portocarero, the Primate

CARDINAL PORTOCARERO

of Spain. "The Cardinal," remarks Macaulay, "was a mere intriguer, and in no sense a statesman. He had acquired in the Court and in the confessional a rare degree of skill in all the tricks by which weak minds are managed. But of the noble science of government, of the sources of national prosperity and the causes of national decay, he knew no more than his master." Portocarero, though himself a Spaniard, was an uncompromising partisan of French interests, and his policy aimed at a gradual banishment of the Spaniards from participation in the government of their own country. Madame des Ursins had juster views, and she perceived that the Cardinal's conduct was rendering both himself and the French whom he supported hateful to the Spaniards.

These two nations, whose common interests now bound them together, differed widely from each other in character and habits. They had been rivals for centuries, and they could not easily forget former prejudices and animosities. In the "Mémoires de Noailles," published in 1777, the Abbé Millot draws a shrewd comparison between the typical French and Spanish character written in a truly impartial spirit. "The Spaniard," he remarks, "is grave, slow of movement, reserved, prone to disguise his feelings rather than to express them, fixed in his opinions and suspicious of those held by foreigners, attached to old customs, indolent and almost effeminate, yet jealous of authority and keenly sensitive where his honour is concerned. . . . The Frenchman is quick, lively, volatile and full of self-confidence, glorying in the power and renown of his king, and vain of his own high breeding and ready wit, which are too often mere external graces; more ready to perceive what is ridiculous or defective, than to recognise what is estimable, in other nations; judging and acting alike with too much precipitation, and impatient of obstacles which cannot be instantly overcome." It required special gifts in a statesman to induce two nations of such widely different temperaments to act together in concord, and Portocarero had none of those gifts.

There was one party in the State which

steadily opposed the Cardinal's policy from patriotic motives. At the head of this party was the Conde di Montellano, a man who enjoyed universal respect. He and his associates had approved of the Bourbon succession, but they wished Philip V. to reign as a true Spaniard, and abhorred the idea that Spain should be governed as a conquered province of France.

Madame des Ursins resolved to strengthen the hands of this essentially national party, and she resolved also to weaken as far as possible the overweening power of the Spanish priesthood. These were bold undertakings for a new comer and a woman, but she was undismayed by the difficulties they presented. Foremost amongst her obstacles stood the mighty Inquisition whose rule had afflicted Spain for more than two hundred years. So great was the terror inspired by its awful and mysterious proceedings that no Spaniard durst converse on the subject. Madame des Ursins broke this benumbing silence and openly espoused the cause of one of its victims. This was a monk named

Friolan Diaz, the confessor of the late King of Spain, who had been thrown into prison upon a charge of practising sorcery upon that monarch. The unfortunate monk had been subjected to torture in order to force him to a confession of guilt, but no such confession had been extorted. The cause was then tried in the Ecclesiastical Courts, and Diaz was declared innocent, but in spite of this declaration the Inquisition still retained its hold upon him. Philip V. had an interview with Mendoza, Archbishop of Segovia, the Grand Inquisitor, and endeavoured to obtain the release of Diaz, but Mendoza gave only a feigned acquiescence to the wishes of the King, and Diaz still remained a close prisoner.

Madame des Ursins aroused public opinion on the subject; her fearless example was followed, and, for the first time since its foundation, the actions of the Inquisition were openly commented upon in the streets of Madrid. The affair terminated in the release of Diaz. It was in vain that the Pope's Nuncio made a formal protest against such a reversal of the decrees of the Holy Inquisition; from henceforth it was known to all that that body must obey the law. Writing of these events a Spanish historian has remarked, "Spain's dark and gloomy night had given place to a dawn full of consolation and hope." This was true, but the author of this first victory over the Inquisition had excited the undying hatred of the "Holy Office" against herself.

Madame des Ursins held just views on the subject of State finances, as the following incident will show. In September 1702 some galleons bearing treasure from the West Indies reached the coast of Spain under an escort of twenty-five French ships of war. Cadiz was the harbour for the West Indian traffic, but the proximity of the English fleet to that port made it necessary for the galleons to seek shelter elsewhere. They therefore put into Vigo harbour. The treasure, consisting of gold, silver, and valuable merchandise, belonged only in part to the State; much of it was the property of private individuals, foreigners as well as Spaniards. Some of these were now reckoned amongst the enemies of the country, and the question of abstract justice in dealing with the treasure was thus rendered somewhat complicated. Spain was sorely in need of money, and Louis XIV., aware of this fact, wrote to his grandson to advise his seizing upon the whole treasure for the use of the State. In order, however, to pacify those of its owners who were loyal to Philip V., the French King suggested that an interest of six per cent. should be paid to them, and a promise given that the property itself should be handed over on the termination of the war.

Madame des Ursins saw the impolicy as well as the danger of such a course of action, and she at once wrote to M. de Torcy (Minister for Foreign Affairs at Versailles) to protest against the measure. She pointed out that should Philip V. seize upon this property, no private property would in future be considered safe, and that in the end both public and private credit would be irretrievably injured. "It was little likely," she observed, "that the State with its impoverished exchequer could pay the promised interest, and still less likely that it would at the end of a long exhausting war be in a position to refund the property itself."

This letter made such an impression upon Louis XIV. that he not only abandoned his own plan, but adopted one suggested by Madame des Ursins.* By this latter arrangement the property in the treasure ships of all persons who were not enemies to the State was to be at once given over to them. The property confiscated was, as usual, to revert to the State, and a further sum of money for pressing expenses was to be raised by means of a tax upon foreign produce.

Whilst this important affair was under discussion Philip was in Italy, and his absence added further delays to the usual slow progress of Spanish transactions. Finally the affair terminated in an unexpected way. The English fleet appeared off Vigo and attacked the French squadron. Whilst the battle raged the galleons slipped their anchors and hurried farther down the gulf with a view of landing the treasure. But before much could be got on shore they

* See François Combes.

were pursued and overtaken by the English. The French and Spanish Admirals, finding that it was impossible to repulse the enemy, gave orders that the cargoes should be thrown into the sea and the galleons set on fire. The loss to the Spaniards is said to have amounted to eight millions of dollars.

Portocarero's persistent advocacy of French interests to the exclusion of those of the Spaniards had created many enemies for the young King. Among these was Don Juan Henriquez of Cabrera, the hereditary Admiral of Castille; one of the most distinguished noblemen in the country. The Admiral had earned the gratitude of the Austro-Spanish monarchy by fighting bravely for it both by land and sea, and had in consequence been made Master of the Horse to Charles II.; but on Philip V. ascending the throne, he had been deprived of that post by Portocarero. This the Admiral bitterly resented, but he abstained from any expressions of anger and, on the contrary, professed the warmest devotion to the new dynasty. He paid especial court to the young Queen and to her Camarera-Mayor. But Madame des Ursins was in no way blinded by his flattery: she saw that he was acting a treacherous part, and that he was ready on the first opportunity to join the party of the Archduke. In a letter to the Maréchale de Noailles she describes him as a man unworthy of confidence, though an agreeable companion.

As time went on it became gradually known that the Admiral was sending the Allies secret information respecting the country's defences. Madame des Ursins urged that measures should be taken to put a stop to such proceedings, and that, if necessary, the Admiral should be arrested. The absence of the King in Italy made the occasion a critical one, and Portocarero and his party, aware of the powerful position of the Admiral and his family, were afraid to act. The Cardinal, however, offered him the post of Ambassador at the French Court, hoping by this means to keep him at a distance from Madrid. The offer was at first declined, the Admiral probably perceiving its motive, and fearing that his embassy might land him in the

Bastille; but finally he accepted the appointment and commenced preparations for his journey to Paris. Madame des Ursins still, however, suspected his intentions, and thinking it well that his movements should be watched, she requested an Irish colonel in the Spanish army named Burke to offer himself and his regiment to the Admiral as an escort. The escort was accepted, since it could not be refused without arousing suspicion. But even this clever artifice did not deter the wily Spaniard from carrying out his purpose. "Having taken a solemn leave of the Court," writes Lord Mahon, "he set out on the road to France, but had only proceeded three days on his journey when a sealed despatch, which he had left behind him for this very purpose, was brought him by express. He read it with an air of surprise; and, turning to his attendants, informed them that he had just received counter-orders from her Majesty . . . and was now instructed to proceed, in the first place, to the Court of Portugal, and attempt to confirm its wavering alliance. Believed and followed by all his suite, he forthwith turned to the left and made for Zamora, where the authorities were deceived by the same pretence and afforded him every facility for passing into Portugal." Soon after his arrival the Admiral persuaded the King of Portugal to join the alliance against the Bourbons. On May 6, 1703, a treaty was signed at Lisbon in which that monarch acknowledged the Archduke of Austria as King of Spain and undertook to vindicate his rights.

A severe blow was thus dealt at the throne of Philip V. Historians have pointed out the fact that Portocarero was in a great measure responsible for it. This was generally felt, and his credit suffered accordingly.

Through the influence of Madame des Ursins the leader of the national party was made President of the Council of Castille and a member of the Junta. By the elevation of Montellano the chief Council of the State was secularised and the power of the priesthood lessened ; while at the same time the Spanish grandees who had been driven from power were placed once more in their rightful positions.

In all these important circumstances Madame des Ursins' influence had steadily gained ground, whilst that of Portocarero had as surely declined. As time went on the change became more and more apparent, until, at last, it was obvious to all that the Cardinal's rule was at an end. A new power had come into being—that of the Camarera-Mayor.

CHAPTER IV

CLOUDS GATHER AND THE STORM BURSTS

MADAME DES URSINS' increasing power was regarded with a jealous eye by the ultra-French party in Madrid, especially by their leader, the French Ambassador, Cardinal d'Estrée. The Cardinal's policy resembled that of Portocarero, and his overweening pride and contemptuous treatment of the Spanish grandees had aroused the strongest feelings of indignation. His conduct towards the King and Queen was equally obnoxious. He affected to hold the King in tutelage, and endeavoured by secret machinations to alienate him from the Queen and to prejudice him against the Princess des Ursins. In these designs he was aided by the King's confessor, an obsequious Jesuit. "But the very means employed to subvert the Princess's influence only served to prove its strength."*

At last Louis XIV. found it advisable to recall Cardinal d'Estrée. The Cardinal was replaced by his nephew, the Abbé d'Estrée, who proved to be a man of weak character and little capacity. "Madame des Ursins," writes St. Simon somewhat maliciously, "contrived to completely bind and gag the poor Abbé d'Estrée. . . . He actually consented to her strange proposal that he, an Ambassador of France, should not write to his Sovereign but in conjunction with herself." The Abbé, however, inwardly chafed under this restriction, and he long endeavoured to elude it, but in vain. At last, to his relief, an unexpected circumstance operated against his all-powerful directress.

Madame des Ursins had a private secretary named d'Aubigny, the son of a procureur of Paris, upon whose fidelity she could safely rely. This man possessed a natural gift of comic humour, and his droll remarks often afforded

* "Kings of Spain of the House of Bourbon." By W. Coxe.

CARDINAL D'ESTRÉE

AN AWKWARD INCIDENT

the lady amusement when she was weary. One evening she conducted Mons. de Louville, one of the ultra-French party, and the Duke de Medina-Cœli into her private saloon in order to converse with them upon some matters of importance. D'Aubigny happened to be in the room, and on Madame des Ursins' entering he, supposing her to be alone, accosted her in a strangely familiar and brusque manner. So rapid was his utterance that she was unable to check his words before they had reached the ears of the astonished courtiers who followed her. D'Aubigny fled from the room, and an awkward pause ensued. No notice was taken of the circumstance at the time, but shortly afterwards Madame des Ursins discovered that the Abbé d'Estrée had, at last, succeeded in sending off a despatch to the French King without her knowledge. The despatch, however, was not suffered to leave Madrid, for the postal officials, probably seeing that it did not bear Madame des Ursins' private mark of approval, promply forwarded it to her. In this document the Abbé, fancying himself safe from the vigilant eyes of the Camarera-Mayor, gave vent to all his feelings of wounded pride and anger. After a series of bitter complaints, he informed his Sovereign that there "was a low kind of person in Madrid named D'Aubigny who was permitted to be present at State conferences, that he was on intimate terms with the Princess des Ursins, and it was confidently believed that she was married to him." The indignation of the lady on reading this statement can easily be imagined. For the moment her accustomed caution forsook her, and she wrote on the margin of the document the words "*pour mariée non.*" She showed the despatch, thus corrected, to the King and Queen, who both approved her conduct; but she also, imprudently, displayed it to some of the courtiers, so that the affair became public. Finally she sent it off to Louis XIV., together with a letter full of complaints against the conduct of his Ambassador. The old King now took offence. He was wounded on his most vulnerable side, for he considered that the sending to him of this mutilated despatch was an act of gross disrespect to his royal person. Whilst in this irritated state of mind the flame of his anger was fanned and kept burning by the family of the D'Estrées and by other enemies of Madame des Ursins. Even the influence of her staunch friend, Madame de Maintenon, was not sufficient to ward off the thunderbolt that was preparing to fall.

Louis resolved to recall the Princess des Ursins. But, aware of the firm position which she held in the esteem and confidence of the young King and Queen of Spain, he felt that it was necessary to act with caution. He wrote to his grandson: "You have hitherto placed your trust in persons who are either incapable or who act from selfish motives. And yet you seem to be wholly occupied with the personal interest of those very individuals, and, at a time when you ought to be taking a wide and lofty view of the affairs of State, you fix your attention upon the cabals of the Princess des Ursins, whose name I am weary of hearing." To the young Queen he wrote: "You are well aware how much I desired that you should have confidence in the Princess des Ursins, and that I used every means to promote that confidence. Nevertheless, I now find that she, forgetting all our common interests, has given herself up to work out her own feelings of personal animosity, and has been engaged for long past in thwarting the actions of those persons to whom we have entrusted the business of our State. If she had been sincerely attached to you, she would have sacrificed her personal enmity, whether well or ill founded, against the Cardinal d'Estrée, instead of bringing you into the quarrel. Persons in our position should rise above the wrangles of private individuals, and should conduct themselves solely in accordance with their own interests and those of their subjects, which are always identical. I must now either recall my Ambassador — thus abandoning you, and leaving the Princess des Ursins to govern your kingdom—or I must recall her. This latter course I believe to be the right one."

Louis despatched a letter to Madame des Ursins herself containing a severe reprimand "for her act of unparalleled effrontery, which had been aimed so directly against the respect due to his person and the secrecy which should be considered inviolable between himself and his Ambassador." Still, for a time, no active measures were taken by the Court of Versailles to oust the Camarera-Mayor. The young Queen warmly espoused her cause, and although Philip V. took but little part in the affair, that little was also on her side. Louis, who feared to provoke his grandson to a refusal to carry out his wishes, advanced warily, knowing that, in the end, he should be able to compass the downfall of the Princess. But in the meantime she appeared to the general lookers-on to have come out of the affair victorious. It is true the Abbé d'Estrée was officially informed of the reprimand which had been sent to her, but he saw his enemy enjoying all her former power, while he himself had become an object of hatred to her friends. All his hopes of revenge were at an end; the position of the Camarera-Mayor seemed to be unassailable. But in reality Louis XIV. was waiting only for the right moment to strike the blow. It came at last. Philip, urged by his grandfather to take the field in person, left Madrid to join the campaign in Portugal. No sooner was he thus removed from the personal influence of his wife than Louis wrote to him, urging in the strongest terms the necessity of the dismissal and banishment of the Princess. At the same time Louis wrote privately to his Ambassador, giving him full directions how to conduct the whole affair and how best to work upon the young King's mind. "Should the King seem inclined to oppose my wishes," writes Louis, "let him understand to what an extent the war, which I am carrying on for the furtherance of his interests, is burdensome to me. You need not say that I shall abandon his cause, for he would not believe it, but you can hint to him that, unless he yields to my desires, I may be tempted, in spite of my affection for his person, to make peace at the expense of Spain; becoming weary of upholding a dynasty whence I derive nothing but annoyance and contradictions. . . . When you have acquainted the king with these sentiments the Duke of Berwick should follow you and speak to him in a similar manner, but you should not be present when he does this.

"We may look confidently for success after such a stroke as this. My own honour, the interests of the King my grandson, and those of the monarchy itself, are at stake."*

Louis now wrote again to the young Queen exhorting her, with a mixture of kingly authority and parental tenderness, to comply without delay with his wishes; and finally he sent a peremptory order to the Princess des Ursins herself to leave Madrid immediately, to quit for ever the territory of Spain, and to retire into Italy.

The Queen was in despair, but Madame des Ursins—how did she act under this sudden and crushing blow? All her force of character now showed itself. She was undismayed by the storm which raged over her head, and while all her friends were crying out at the injustice done to her and lamenting her fate,

* See "Mémoires de Noailles."

she alone remained calm and collected. Her eyes were opened to the whole plot that had been laid against her. She understood now why the catastrophe had been delayed, and saw that her triumph had been a fictitious one. Madame des Ursins allowed herself no vain delusions, but faced the facts bravely. Submission for the time being, she saw, was the only course open to her; but her submission was in every way dignified. She requested but one favour of the King of France, namely, the delay of a few days in order to allow time for the necessary preparations for her long journey. This delay granted, she made use of it with consummate skill and forethought to prepare a way for her ultimate return to power. She gave the Queen minute instructions respecting her future conduct, unfolding for her, at the same time, the characters of the persons with whom she would have to deal, and showing her what would be the wisest course to pursue to facilitate their future reunion. She selected for her successor as Camarera-Mayor the Duchess de Monteillano, a lady of an amiable disposition but of limited capacity, one whom she would have little difficulty in setting aside when occasion required; and she finally engaged a lady of the Court who was especially devoted to her interests to become her regular correspondent, and to give her exact information of all that took place at Madrid during her absence. "In a word," says St. Simon, "she arranged all her machinery, and, under the pretext of unavoidable delays in the preparations for her journey, she remained quietly at Madrid whilst the couriers from Versailles, bringing her peremptory orders to depart, were redoubled. She would not quit the field until she had matured and established her whole plan of operations. Madame des Ursins found time to pay farewell visits to all her friends and acquaintances, and she took occasion to inform them that the only regret she felt in leaving Madrid was in parting with the Queen. She observed a strict silence respecting the ill treatment she had received, and bore it with a courage and firmness that evinced neither arrogance, on the one hand, which might irritate her opponents, nor, on the other, the slightest tinge of meanness."

When, at last, Madame des Ursins took her departure from the Spanish capital she was escorted by the Queen for two leagues on her route. She received every mark of distinguishing attention, and the Queen took scrupulous care to display to every one the perfect confidence that subsisted between them. Madame des Ursins had fixed upon the town of Alcala, not many miles distant from Madrid, for her first halting-place. After remaining there for five weeks and employing that period to the best advantage in furthering her interests, she resumed her journey. In all her letters to her friends at Versailles the only mitigation of her sentence of banishment which she urged them to obtain for her was that the country of her exile should be France instead of Italy. Once established within reach of Versailles, she felt that the issue of events could be moulded by her genius for diplomacy. "Although she had little expectation of this favour being immediately granted," writes St. Simon, "her courage

A CONFIDENT DIPLOMATIST

never wavered. Experience of life at Court proves (as she well knew) that there all things pass away with time, even the most terrible storms, for him who does not abandon his own cause through vexation and disappointment."

But, for the moment, Madame des Ursins' prospects must have seemed very gloomy. She had been publicly disgraced and was now an exile, whilst her enemies, the D'Estrées, laden with honours by the French King, triumphed in her fall. She was by no means blind to the machinations of Louis to prevent the possibility of her return to power. The Duc de Grammont had been appointed to succeed the Abbé d'Estrée as French Ambassador at Madrid. He was, like his predecessors, a partisan of French interests, and was therefore entirely opposed to the policy pursued by the Princess des Ursins. His special mission, though a secret one, was to undermine her influence in every possible way, and to inspire Philip V. with a desire to rule, independently, on his own account. The Duke was full of confidence in his own powers, and seemed to think that success was certain. He had no sooner crossed the frontier than he wrote to M. de Torcy (Minister for Foreign Affairs at Versailles): "I can see at a glance that prosperity for Spain can only be obtained by the King [of France] ruling that country despotically. Spain must not be allowed to suspect that he does so, but this we can easily manage."

The Duke encountered the Princess des Ursins at Vittoria. He had received instructions to call upon her and to treat her politely, but to avoid any discussion of her affairs. He therefore eluded all her questions by feigning a total ignorance of her disgrace. He played his part so well that the lady, although detecting the imposture, complimented him on his diplomacy, remarking, "You are well suited to your post, for you possess the first qualification of an ambassador—secrecy."*

Arrived at Madrid the Duke was charmed with his first formal reception by the King and Queen. He was equally pleased at the

* "Mémoires de Noailles."

assurance expressed by the Abbé d'Estrée that "all would go well now that the Princess des Ursins had been banished, and that the Queen's affection for her would soon expire." The morning after his arrival, however, his confidence received a severe shock. The Queen, in a private interview, demanded an explanation of the outrage perpetrated against the Princess des Ursins. She spoke with indignation of the treatment her friend had received, and pointed to the fact that it involved an insult, not only to the lady herself, but to the King and Queen of Spain, who had placed their full confidence in her. At the close of the conference the Queen burst into tears, and the Duke, who had already publicly condemned the conduct of the Princess, was utterly confounded. He knew not what to say, and made but a sorry figure before this injured and warm-hearted girl of sixteen.

Louis XIV., on being informed by his Ambassador of the Queen's sentiments, became fearful lest she should urge him to restore Madame des Ursins to power. He considered that compliance with such a request would be impossible, and he dreaded, above all things, an open rupture between the Courts of France and Spain. He judged it expedient, therefore, to take measures to prevent such an application, and with this view he wrote to M. de Chateauneuf, a Frenchman holding a high post at Madrid (July 10, 1704): "Make the Queen clearly understand that my resolution of recalling the Princess des Ursins was not taken without long and mature consideration; and that the reasons which moved me to take that step were so powerful as to make it impossible for me to change my mind. Tell the Queen that I have been in no way influenced by the intrigues and cabals of the Princess's enemies, and inform her that I decide all matters for myself, and that no one dares to imagine that I allow myself to be biassed by false reports." *

The Duc de Grammont found his task more and more difficult, and his despatches to Versailles reflect his doubts and perplexities. One day he counsels Louis to assume a more

* See "Mémoires de Noailles."

authoritative tone towards the Court of Spain and to display "*les grosses dents*"; a few days later he advises him to adopt a conciliatory attitude and to proceed gently as if with a "*patte de velours.*" But whatever course the French King pursued, he found that an obstacle had arisen to all cordial relations between him and his grandson. The fact was that though Philip had yielded to the pressure put upon him respecting the dismissal of the Princess des Ursins, he had done so merely because he felt that opposition was vain. The affair had caused him much annoyance, and he was especially grieved at the sorrow it had occasioned to his wife, to whom her loss was irremediable.

The estrangement between the Kings of France and Spain was especially inconvenient, coming as it did at a time when they were surrounded by enemies and when their common interests demanded prompt and decisive action. Their difficulties had been largely increased by the defection of the Duke of Savoy, father of the young Queen of Spain, who was now fighting on the side of Austria. One disaster followed another. Gibraltar was wrested from the Spanish crown; a revolt had broken out in Catalonia; and the Archduke had been proclaimed King of Spain by the Allies under the title of Charles III.

Whilst these various events were taking place Madame des Ursins' friends at the French Court were beginning to feel the inconvenience to themselves of her disgrace. Madame de Maintenon felt it especially, for she had lost the means of obtaining secret and sure information as to the course of affairs in Spain and as to the conduct of the French Ambassadors. She now determined to bring about, if possible, the alteration in the sentence of banishment desired by her friend. But even her powerful influence was barely sufficient to induce the irritated monarch to make the concession. At last, however, it was made, and the Princess des Ursins received permission to take up her residence at Toulouse.

The next favour the Princess desired to obtain was permission for a private interview with Louis XIV. in order that she might explain and justify her conduct. She was well aware that time must elapse before this permission would be granted, but she already began to perceive the probability of a change of affairs in her favour. She was careful, however, to show no signs of her rising hopes. On the contrary, she spoke continually to her acquaintance at Toulouse of her approaching return to Rome, "where she looked forward to enjoying to the full a life of retirement and repose, where she could listen to her favourite Italian music, and where she intended to drink asses' milk."

As time went on, the old King's anger began gradually to subside. His pride had been appeased by the results which had followed his displeasure. The Princess's downfall had been sudden and sure. Even her friends had not dared to defend her; all had bowed submissively to his authority. There was consolation in these reflections, and the affair had, therefore, ceased to exasperate him. When this change in the King's sentiments became apparent to the watchful friends of the Princess, they saw that the time had arrived when they might venture to plead for a personal interview.

One of these friends was the Archbishop of Aix, a man skilled in diplomatic intrigues and who possessed an intimate knowledge of the King's character and habits of mind. The Archbishop, St. Simon tells us, undertook to break the ice. He artfully ushered in the subject by speaking, with concern, of the "abyss of humiliation" into which "a single act of folly had precipitated the unfortunate lady." He went on to describe, in exaggerated terms, her grief at having offended the King and her mortification "at not being allowed to explain her conduct." "Her situation was especially to be deplored," concluded his Grace, "since the main object of her mission in Spain had been to secure obedience to his Majesty's behests, and in every possible way to afford him satisfaction." As these remarks were suffered to pass unchallenged, the Archbishop returned to the charge again and again. He

SAINT SIMON

was supported on the one hand by the Marquis d'Harcourt, who had originally accompanied Philip V. to Spain as his chief counsellor, and on the other hand, by Madame de Maintenon. At this stage of affairs a letter arrived from the young Queen of Spain to her grandfather, urging, in earnest but dignified terms, the same suit. Louis now yielded to the pressure put upon him and consented to give the desired audience.

No sooner were the words of acquiescence fairly pronounced than a courier was despatched in all haste to Toulouse, bearing the royal mandate. The lady's joy on its receipt can easily be imagined; but Madame des Ursins, "ever mistress of herself," was "no more shaken by this sudden prospect of a brilliant future than she had been by the fall of the thunderbolt at Madrid."* Her judgment remained cool and collected. She recognised the critical position of her affairs and saw that a false move would be fatal. The King still "frowned on her and stood upon his guard."

* St. Simon.

His pride must not be wounded nor his suspicions of her ultimate designs aroused. In spite, therefore, of her high hopes, she still retained the air of a person suffering under disgrace and humiliation, and she instructed her friends to adopt the same tone on her behalf.

Madame des Ursins had much to do before leaving Toulouse. Diplomatic letters, furthering her interests both in France and Spain, had to be written; in which, we are told, she displayed "an admirable presence of mind." Plans also had to be formed for her own future conduct. In fixing a time for her departure she showed her usual tact. She would not hurry it lest she should appear unduly eager to avail herself of the King's permission, but, on the other hand, she was careful not to delay it so long as to seem indifferent to the royal favour. Finally, towards the end of December 1704, Madame des Ursins quitted the place of her exile and commenced her journey to Paris.

CHAPTER V

FORTUNE'S CHANGES

"No sooner," writes St. Simon, "had the courier left Paris with the important despatch for Madame des Ursins than a rumour began to circulate of her expected arrival, a rumour which a few days later was publicly confirmed. The commotion which this intelligence produced at Court is almost inconceivable. Every one was on the alert, perceiving that the arrival of so important a personage augured some strange turn of events. All made ready, as it were, to salute a rising sun which would change the face of nature. People who had never so much as uttered her name before now boasted of her friendship and claimed congratulations on her advent. Others, who had actually been in league with her enemies, were not ashamed to affect transports of joy and to pay the meanest homage in those quarters where it would appear as incense offered to the Princess.

"The Duke of Alva, who had formerly judged it expedient to ally himself firmly with the D'Estrée faction, now endeavoured to atone for that error by lavishing upon Madame des Ursins the most flattering attentions." When on Sunday, January 4, 1705, she was approaching Paris, "he drove many miles beyond the city, accompanied by the Duchess of Alva and his suite, to meet her on the road. Many other people of distinction also went out to meet her. The Duke conducted the lady in state to his own mansion, where she passed the first night and where he gave a fête in her honour." It was with much reluctance that he suffered his guest to depart the following day, but upon this she insisted in order to take up her residence with Madame d'Egmont, the niece of her staunch friend the Archbishop of Aix.

"A prodigious concourse of people went to pay their court to Madame des Ursins, impelled by curiosity, hope, fear, or fashion. M. le

Prince was among the first to go, and his example was followed by all the distinguished officers of the Court, whether they had been previously acquainted with her or not.

"From this time forward Madame des Ursins changed her tone. She now became aware that, instead of having to sustain the part of an accused person as she had expected, she might herself become the accuser, and demand justice in the face of those persons who . . . had brought upon her such dire ill usage and who had caused her to be regarded by two great nations as disgraced and humiliated.

"The King (who had been at Marly)" continues St. Simon, "returned to Versailles on Saturday, January 10, and Madame des Ursins arrived there the same day. She stayed at the house of D'Alègre. I went at once to call upon her. We had always kept up our intercourse, and I had received, on many occasions, marks of her regard. I was well received, but I had expected to be treated with less reserve than she at first evinced. Presently Harcourt, who had delayed until then to pay his respects, entered the room, and I felt it would be wise to retire. On rising to take my leave, Madame des Ursins stopped me to make a few friendly remarks, and at once resuming all her former openness of manner, observed that 'she promised herself the pleasure of soon seeing me again, and of being able then to converse with me more at her ease.' I noticed that Harcourt was surprised at this. On quitting the house I saw Torcy* entering.

". . . The following day (Sunday) Madame des Ursins, arrayed in sumptuous attire, repaired to the palace for her interview with the King. She remained with him *tête-à-tête* for two hours and a half. Thence she proceeded to pay a call of some length on the Duchess of Burgundy; and the next morning held a long private conference with Madame de Maintenon. On the Tuesday she again returned to the palace, and remained closeted for a great while with both the King and Madame de Maintenon. . . . So many private audiences, attended evidently with marked success, produced a

* Minister for Foreign Affairs.

great effect at Versailles, and much increased the general eagerness to pay court to Madame des Ursins."

The King and Queen of Spain were not slow in evincing their joy at the happy turn of events. They "sent an envoy to Louis XIV. for the express purpose of conveying their thanks for his favourable reception of the Princess. At the same time they desired their Ambassador, the Duke of Alva, to pay her a visit of ceremony, accompanied by his whole retinue, an honour usually paid only to princesses of the blood royal."

About this time the Court removed to Marly, where Madame des Ursins was invited to become the King's guest. St. Simon was of the party. He writes: "Apartments were given to her in the 'Avenue' . . . . Nothing could exceed the King's watchful solicitude to do her honour. It could not have been greater had she been the queen of some foreign country on her first visit to his Court. As soon as Madame des Ursins made her appearance he became entirely engrossed by her. He entertained her with conversation, pointed out objects of interest, asked for her opinion and sought her approval with an air of flattering gallantry." All this attention rendered her "the divinity of the Court; and the servile homage that she received from all persons, however exalted their rank or official position, can hardly be imagined. Her very looks were counted, and a remark from her lips to ladies of the highest standing would throw them into ecstacies of delight."

Even St. Simon himself expresses his satisfaction at the pleasant footing upon which both he and his wife stood with Madame des Ursins. "I used to go and see her," he writes, "nearly every morning. I avoided the hours when she received official visits. We chatted together with our usual ease and freedom, and she gave me information upon many matters of interest. I learnt from her the private opinions held by the King and Madame de Maintenon concerning many people. I was flattered at this mark of confidence from the dictatress of the Court. Our intimacy was noticed by all, and it brought me a sudden and unusual amount of deference. Whenever Madame des Ursins met Madame de St. Simon she accosted her in complimentary terms and was solicitous to introduce her into any agreeable conversation that might be going on. Sometimes she would lead my wife up to a mirror and rearrange part of her dress or coiffure, just as she might have done for a daughter of her own. The bystanders asked each other with astonishment, and many with feelings of envy, whence sprang this great friendship of which no one had suspected the existence?"

Several balls were given during the visit of the Princess des Ursins. St. Simon informs us that the "King and Queen of England" were often at the Marly balls. By these titles he designates the first Pretender and his mother, the widow of James II. Since the former had been publicly recognised by Louis XIV., he was received with royal honours. He and his sister always opened the ball, and as soon as the dance commenced the old King would rise from his state chair and remain standing until it was concluded. This dance was probably the "pavane" (peacock). It was a dance of ceremony and was performed to a slow and stately measure. The dancers were in full dress. Judges, and other dignitaries of high standing, wore their robes of office, and the princes of the blood royal wore their swords and their long mantles. As these gentlemen bowed to their partners the points of their swords lifted up their mantles behind, giving somewhat the appearance of a peacock's tail. Hence the name of the dance.

Madame de Maintenon, who rarely made her appearance at festive gatherings, came to these balls in honour of her friend the Princess des Ursins. These two ladies occupied the highest places of honour, being seated on either side of the King. The conversation between the three never flagged. "Conversation," says Madame de Staël, "to the French is as it were a musical instrument upon which they delight to play." This was eminently the case with the Princess des Ursins. The King was captivated by her grace and lively talents. She appreciated

THE PRETENDER, STYLED "JACQUES III., ROI D'ANGLETERRE," AGED 16 YEARS

fully his intellectual gifts; and even Madame de Maintenon, usually so sedate and reserved, seemed, for the moment, to grow young again.

A circumstance occurred at one of these balls which created no small sensation. "Madame des Ursins," writes St. Simon, "entered the saloon carrying under her arm a lap-dog, just as she might have done in the privacy of her own parlour. The company were amazed beyond measure at such an act of temerity, an act which not even the Duchess of Burgundy herself would have ventured to perform. Their amazement was not diminished when they observed the King turning frequently to the lady to caress the dog. Never till then," adds the chronicler, "had a subject attained to such a giddy height in royal favour."

When, during the period of Madame des Ursins' disgrace, Louis XIV. gave his consent to a personal interview with the lady, St. Simon foresaw the inevitable result of that step. He remarks that "the King, to whom the truth never penetrated, imprisoned as he was in a charmed circle of his own creating, was probably the only individual within the two kingdoms who had no suspicion that the appearance of Madame des Ursins at his Court must be the sure pledge of her return to Spain, and of her return endowed with a power still greater than before." The discovery, however, about fifty years ago, by M. Geffroy, of a curious secret correspondence proves that the old King was fully aware of the consequence of his act. He was far too shrewd and clear-sighted to be misled; and it is evident that he merely "played the comedy" of relenting. This secret correspondence was carried on, during the period of Madame des Ursins' banishment, between the King and the Duc de Grammont, then French Ambassador at Madrid. The Duke's special mission, as has been already stated, was to undermine the influence of Madame des Ursins and to inspire Philip V. with a desire to rule his dominions on his own account. The Duke reports to his Sovereign his various endeavours to compass that object, and Louis, in his replies, gives his Ambassador directions for his conduct. The King's letters are not in his own handwriting, but "they contain without doubt," observes M. Geffroy, "his thoughts and views and the secret orders which he did not choose to convey in the ordinary official documents." Pseudonyms are substituted for proper names. They vary continually, but a key to their meaning fortunately exists, the Duke having himself written explanations between the lines. The letters are also docketed by him. On one of his own are the words: "Au roi sous le nom de M. de la Graingaudière," and on one of the King's, "Du roi sous le nom de baron de la Roquerie," and on another of the King's "Sous le nom de Lespine Blanche." The French King is referred to as "l'ami," Philip V. as "la bonté," his wife as "l'esprit," and Madame des Ursins as "la confidente." As time goes on the tone of the royal letters gradually changes respecting the Princess des Ursins, and in March, 1705, after her reception at Versailles, Louis writes (under the name of Des Laurens): "L'ami has always believed that you were mistaken in your judgment of 'la bonté,' and that he will never have sufficient force of character to resist 'l'esprit.' This circumstance has made it necessary to adopt the course of sending 'la confidente' back [to Madrid]."

The complete failure of the Duc de Grammont's mission had convinced Louis of the "absolute incapacity of Philip V. to govern on his own account." It had also convinced him of Philip's entire dependence on his wife and of his wife's devotion to Madame des Ursins—a devotion which neither separation nor the degradation of the Princess had been able to weaken. Whilst her friend was suffering under disgrace and banishment, the indignation of the Queen against Louis had frustrated French influence in Spain, and it had become evident to the mind of the King of France that if amicable relations between the two countries were to be restored, Madame des Ursins must return to power. Here, then, is to be found the reason which induced Louis to withdraw his displeasure and to receive the lady at Versailles. He looked upon this act as an irksome necessity. But no sooner had Madame des

Ursins arrived at Court than a further change affected the King's mind.

"Louis," remarks Ste. Beuve, "had expected to find in the ex-Camarera-Mayor an intriguing woman of the Fronde type . . . instead of this he found a person endowed, indeed, by nature with a capacity to command, but who also shone brilliantly in society. Madame des Ursins achieved an intellectual triumph." And, describing the intercourse between her, the King, and Madame de Maintenon, he continues: "Of these three, if I may dare to say so, the Princess des Ursins had the most complete mastery of the situation. Her quick intelligence had seized upon every point at issue, and, being least bound to play a part, she played hers the best."

Month after month passed by, and Madame des Ursins still continued to reside at the French Court. People began to wonder why she did not return to Spain. St. Simon tells us that she had some thoughts of settling herself permanently at Versailles, with a view of succeeding to the position of Madame de

Maintenon as wife to the King on the death of that lady. But there is no proof that she entertained such an idea, and Ste. Beuve does not give credence to the supposition. She was evidently waiting for the best opportunity to make her own conditions respecting her return to Madrid.

Affairs in Spain were becoming more and more critical, and at last a time arrived when Madame des Ursins was urged to return to power. She now hung back, and gave expression to doubts and scruples. She "felt reluctance," she remarked, "to assume a post of such power and responsibility in a country which she had quitted with all the ignominy of a supposed criminal." She pointed out the fact that, however desirous she might be to serve the Kings of France and Spain, success would be unattainable unless some marks of signal favour and approval were publicly accorded to her as evidence of the high authority under which she acted. She acknowledged that she "felt herself almost overpowered by the continued marks of royal favour bestowed upon her during her residence at the French Court, but these were done in private, and the knowledge of them could not reach the Spanish nation." In short, "her grace, her eloquence, her happy turn of expressions, her wit, her tact—all contributed to produce a result which surpassed even her expectations." *

In a private conference between the King, Madame de Maintenon, and the Princess des Ursins which took place at Marly on June 15, 1705, the conditions were finally agreed upon and a treaty signed. This treaty, M. Geffroy tells us, was deposited in the hands of Madame de Maintenon, who alludes to it in a letter to her friend, written two years later. "I have still in my casket," she remarks, "the treaty containing the articles which you drew up in my room at Marly."

The result of this treaty was as follows. The King promised that henceforth no credence should be given at Versailles to any reports, whether verbal or by letter, censuring the administration of the Princess des Ursins.

* St. Simon.

The Princess was, on her return to Madrid, to be free to choose such persons for Ministers as would be most likely to act in accordance with her views. She was also to be free at all times to adopt or reject, as she deemed best, the recommendations made by the French Ambassadors.

The King granted the Princess des Ursins an additional pension of 20,000 livres and also gave her 30,000 to defray the expenses of her journey.

Her elder brother, M. de Noirmoutier, who was afflicted with blindness and who led a retired life, was created a Duke in his own right; and her second brother, the Abbé de la Trimouille, was created a Cardinal; the King making certain concessions to the Pope in order to obtain this favour for the Princess.

Thus, laden with honours, Madame des Ursins at last took her leave of the French Court. "This was the woman," exclaims St. Simon, "whose downfall the King had so ardently desired," and which "he congratulated himself he had so effectually compassed!"

CHAPTER VI

A SPANISH OVATION

THE journey of Madame des Ursins from Paris to Madrid resembled a royal progress. Her last French resting-place was the ancient fishing town of St. Jean-de-Luz, nestling on a spur of the Pyrenees. Here the royal Spanish equipages with a crowd of Spanish nobles had crossed the border to receive her. So we are told by the *Mércure Galant*, a periodical of the day. At each town through which she passed she was received in state at the city gates, addresses of welcome were presented to her and fêtes given in her honour. The *Mércure Galant* goes on to say, "Dances, games, bull-fights, fireworks, and cannonades celebrated her return to Spain. At Vittoria, which is more than sixty leagues from Madrid, the Princess was met by an equerry, at the head of a cortège sent by the Queen Dowager to swell her retinue and to accompany her to Madrid. Honours multiplied as she approached the capital, but they culminated on the last day of her journey, when she reached Canillas, a village two leagues from Madrid. Here the King and Queen had sent their 'officiers de bouche' to prepare a magnificent banquet, and here the Princess des Ursins was received by the French Ambassador, by Marshal Tessé, by several foreign Ministers, and by a prodigious number of grandees." Strange to say, the heroine of all this ovation could not be present at this banquet given in her honour, as the rules of Spanish Court etiquette forbade women to eat in the presence of men. The Princess, therefore, partook of the repast in the privacy of her own apartment; whilst the French Ambassador and Marshal Tessé did the honours of the feast. "At half-past five o'clock their Majesties the King and Queen, accompanied by the whole Court, arrived to welcome her." We fancy we see the brilliant gathering—the cavaliers with laced coats and shining cuirasses on their Flemish steeds, the ladies in their heavy gilded coaches drawn by teams of horses or mules whose long silken traces mark the traveller of distinction and are kept from entanglement by the running lackies.

"The Princess des Ursins met their Majesties at their carriage door. The King and Queen kissed her on both cheeks, and evinced in every possible way their joy on the occasion. . . . On leaving Canillas their Majesties invited the Princess to ride with them in their own carriage; but as it is forbidden by etiquette for any one to enter the Queen's carriage when the King is with her, she declined this honour, and begged their Majesties to permit her, on this single occasion, to disobey them. The Princess des Ursins then took her seat in the official carriage prepared for the use of the Camarera-Mayor, and followed immediately behind the royal equipage. Thus she resumed possession of a post to which she had been already recalled by the acclamations of the people."

A contemporary Spanish historian, "the

grave Marquess di San Phélipe," recounting the above events, observes that, "while receiving these high marks of distinction, so rarely paid by Sovereigns to their subjects, the Princess des Ursins was complete mistress of herself," and that "she wisely endeavoured, by her attitude of deep respect towards their Majesties, to moderate the effect produced upon the lookers-on by their outspoken expressions of royal favour."

Full and particular accounts of the reception of the Princess were sent to Louis XIV. both by his Ambassador and by Marshal Tessé, who commanded the French forces in Spain. The Marshal, after giving the same details that we have quoted from the *Mércure Galant*, begs leave to relate to his Majesty a laughable incident of Spanish etiquette, which he thinks may amuse the young Duchess of Burgundy. One of the maids of honour, who had accompanied the Queen to Canillas, was to be married the following day. A Court rule established by Charles V. or Philip II. required that a lady in such circumstances should weep the whole of the last day of her life in the palace. "This girl," writes the Marshal, "felt herself therefore bound to cry, and did her utmost to do so; at the same time she wished to appear joyful at the return of Madame des Ursins, and the result was a most comical struggle in her countenance between mirth and melancholy, which made us nearly die of laughing."

Madame des Ursins' triumph was rendered complete by the following letter from Louis XIV. to the Queen of Spain, written September 20, 1705. After responding to some expressions of affectionate interest in his own concerns, the King remarks to his grand-daughter : " The Princess des Ursins will leave you in no doubt of my sentiments towards you. I learn with feelings of sincere pleasure of your joy at her return, and of that joy being continually renewed. I am persuaded that her excellent sense, and the confidence which you place in her, will contribute greatly to improve the condition of affairs."

Madame des Ursins had inaugurated some important political changes even before she re-entered Spain. At one of the many private conferences held between herself, Louis XIV., and Madame de Maintenon, it had been resolved that the Duc de Grammont should be recalled from Madrid. But before any measures could be taken the Duke sent in his resignation. He had found his task a hopeless one; and even whilst he was doing his utmost to undermine the influence of Madame des Ursins he had felt her value. Although she was then in exile and in disgrace, he wrote to *her* as the person most capable of rendering service to the country, and, after complaining of the system of government in Spain, he had made use of this expression: "Get this system changed. People have confidence in you."

The Duke's successor had already been chosen by Madame des Ursins. This was Amelot, Marquis de Gournay, a man who possessed a high reputation for successful diplomacy and with whom the lady was well acquainted. Amelot reached Madrid before the arrival of the Princess des Ursins. The latter wrote to Madame de Maintenon, whilst yet on her journey: "I already know, generally speaking, that affairs are going well as regards he conduct of the war and the personal safety of their Majesties.

"I saw a brother of Marshal Villars yesterday, who assured me a great change for the better has been remarked since the arrival of M. Amelot and the Sieur Orry. They have rendered a signal service to the State in stemming, even for a time, the torrent which was hurrying the monarchy to its ruin. But you will see still greater things accomplished before long . . . M. Amelot's zeal for his King is untainted by motives of self-interest. He will promote cordial intercourse between the two monarchs, and their union, which is of such vital importance, will be strengthened. Indeed, all things must prosper in the hands of an Ambassador who is himself free from evil passions and who is an enemy to all intrigue."

During the late feeble government, when traitors had grown bold by impunity, the Marquis de Liganez, a powerful grandee, had been carrying on secret negotiations with the

Austrian party. The Marquis was now arrested. "The arrest and imprisonment of the Marquis de Liganez," writes Madame des Ursins, "has been successfully carried through. This blow was necessary in order to re-establish the King of Spain's authority; and you have every reason to augur well of M. Amelot's embassy, which begins with a measure so wise and so bold."

From this time the Princess des Ursins corresponded regularly with Madame de Maintenon. The readers of her letters cannot fail to be struck by their *modern* style. They contain neither obsolete words nor pedantic expressions such as we find in English letters of that period. Compare, for instance a letter of Lord Peterborough's with one of Madame des Ursins' both written from Spain under the same date. One belongs to a past world, the other to the world of to-day. This modern freshness of style is a distinguishing feature of the best French letters of a still earlier date; notably of Madame de Sévigné's. One cause of this lies in the fact that the French language has changed comparatively little during the last two hundred and fifty years. Modern French was modelled, so to speak, in the seventeenth century, and modelled largely by women; a fact the more singular since, "with few exceptions, women of rank and good breeding scarcely knew how to spell." They felt this inconvenience and were determined to remove it. "In one of their literary assemblies a Madame Leroi told Leclerc (secretary of the French Academy) that *spelling must be altered*, so that women could write correctly as well as men; and that words should be written as they were pronounced. To this sensible, though revolutionary proposal M. Leclerc politely acceded. He took a pen, Madame de Ladurandière took a book, and Mesdames Leroi and de St. Loup decided what letters should be omitted and what retained in the words which she read and he wrote. A long list of the words thus improved has been preserved by Somaise, the narrator of the anecdote."* "These literary ladies—'Précieuses,' as they were called—numbered, at one time, more than eight

* See "French Women of Letters," by Julia Kavanagh.

hundred. They were divided into cycles, each cycle having a distinct life of its own." Molière has ridiculed them, and doubtless there was a comic element in their proceedings, but nevertheless they did a good work for French literature. "For depravity and impure language, whether spoken or written, they substituted the refinement of virtue and the delicacy of good taste."*

Soon after the Princess des Ursins' re-establishment in Madrid, an opportunity occurred for the disposal of a post of considerable importance, that of Majordomo-Major, which had become vacant by the death of the Marquis de Villafranca. The Duke of Alva had long coveted the post, and with a view to securing it had paid assiduous court to Madame des Ursins ever since her return to favour at Versailles. The Duke's rank, his high official position, his long services, all seemed to point him out as the fittest person to be the new Majordomo-Major, and besides all this Louis XIV. approved his claims. But Madame des

* See "French Women of Letters," by Julia Kavanagh.

Ursins had other views. "The attachment which the Duke of Alva had at one time evinced for the D'Estrées," remarks St. Simon, "could not be effaced from her memory, and it cost him this great appointment."

Madame des Ursins' choice fell upon the Duke de Frias, the High Constable of Castile. This man had experienced some causes of annoyance since the advent of the French dynasty; notably in not being created Commander-in-Chief of the Forces, a post which he considered to be his due. He was known to have felt this disappointment so keenly that he was suspected of secretly favouring the cause of the Archduke. By conferring upon the Duke de Frias such a distinction as the post in question, Madame des Ursins knew she should bind him securely to the interests of Philip V., and that, in addition, his powerful name would serve as a means of rallying round the young King many other grandees of wavering loyalty. For her own part she would gain for an ally a person of high distinction at the Court of Madrid, and one who, since he owed his brilliant position entirely to her influence, would be prepared to act in accordance with her views.

The Duke of Berwick was at the head of the Spanish army, which had been increased in size by a French contingent. The Duke was a son of James II. by Arabella Churchill, a sister of the Duke of Marlborough. "In these two great soldiers the Churchills have the singular honour of having produced the most formidable antagonist and the ablest defender of the throne of France." *

We have already spoken of the loss of Gibraltar in 1704. Since then a vigorous attempt had been made by the French and Spaniards to wrest the rock from the English; but without success. As is well known, from henceforth this "important key to the Mediterranean" was secured to England. The Archduke Charles, now proclaimed King of Spain by the Allies, had been carrying on the war from the side of Portugal. He now set sail, escorted by the British fleet, and landed near

* See Kitchin's "History of France."

THE ARCHDUKE CHARLES, REPRESENTED AS CHARLES III. OF SPAIN

A RIVAL KING

Barcelona, where he was met by an English army under the command of the celebrated Earl of Peterborough. The Catalonians received the Archduke joyfully, for he had promised to respect their ancient privileges, a promise they had been unable to obtain from Philip. The inhabitants of Barcelona compelled the garrison to throw open its gates to Charles, the province hailed him as King, and its example was followed by Valencia and Aragon.

"We have lost Barcelona, Madame!" writes the Princess des Ursins to Madame de Maintenon (October 30, 1705). "This disaster renders the immediate succour of France absolutely necessary. . . . We learn that the greater part of the garrison have consented to join the army of the enemy. . . . The evil increases every moment, and there is none under God to whom we can look for help save to the King."

In another letter she remarks: "The Portuguese are mustering fresh troops, whilst the Spaniards, who are urged in every possible way to join the army, refuse to enlist. They satisfy their consciences by declaring valiantly that they will shed the last drop of their blood for their Majesties, but in the meantime they will not run the risk of shedding the first drop."

She writes to M. de Torcy, Minister for Foreign Affairs at Versailles (November 6): "The troubles which threaten us are far greater than you appear to be aware of, judging from the letter with which you have honoured me. It is impossible for us, unaided by France, to arrest the fury of the rebellion. One course only remains for us to adopt. I will enter into that subject when I have replied to those articles in your letter which demand explanation. . . . It is a well-known fact, sir, and one which cannot be controverted, that this nation accepted a French prince for their King solely because they feared that the Emperor was not sufficiently powerful to protect them. The League at that time was disunited, and the House of Austria seemed to be abandoned by her allies, who were loudly demanding the division of the kingdom. France, on the other hand, had powerful armies all along the frontiers of Spain. Here, then, is to be found the main argument used by those who counselled Charles II. to make a will in favour of the Duke of Anjou. Philip V. was received with acclamations of joy; and not a single subject, whether of high or low degree, appeared to be discontented so long as affairs remained in the same condition. But ever since the chief part of Europe has declared in favour of the Archduke, the French have ceased to be upon a secure footing in Madrid. The defection of the Duke of Savoy, and our reverses on the frontiers of Portugal, have tended to shake still further the confidence of the Spanish people; but what has affected them most of all is the disastrous event of Hochstet,* which they regard as the last fatal blow that will ruin France.

"The Archduke may reach Aragon before the end of this month with twenty thousand men. We must not count upon the inhabitants offering any resistance. The King of Spain

* Battle of Blenheim.

cannot leave garrisons in unfortified towns, or he would run the risk of losing his best troops; nor can we with only eight thousand men arrest the progress of an enemy so superior in numbers. The least defeat might terrify the people of Madrid, and their Catholic Majesties, finding themselves no longer in a place of safety, would have no course open to them but that of a humiliating flight, a course which would inevitably seal the fate of Spain.

"Under the present circumstances it appears to me that the King should desire Marshal Tessé to march as soon as possible to this part of the country with all the French soldiers at his command, and that the Marshal should hand over the defence of the Portuguese frontiers to some of the Spanish troops. The Spaniards, it seems, will not surrender themselves to the Portuguese in the cowardly manner they have done to the Archduke. They would, therefore, suffice, during the winter months, to prevent the enemy from penetrating into this country, especially if a few regiments of cavalry were left behind. If this plan were carried out, the King of Spain could command an army numbering, with his own and the French troops, at least twenty thousand men, and with it he could enter Catalonia, disarm its inhabitants, and force the enemy to retreat to Barcelona.

"I am well aware that this course offers some disadvantages, but any other would offer many more. We shall lose all, to a certainty, if we refuse to make some sacrifice now."

Madame des Ursins writes to Chamillart, Louis XIV.'s Minister of War (November 20): "I have the honour of informing you, sir, that I consider your being so ill informed regarding the affairs of this country as a grave evil. It is impossible for you to inaugurate just measures if you are not thoroughly conversant with the facts of the case.

"The plan which you have sent to M. Amelot is based upon the theory that the campaign in Catalonia is now at an end, and that the Archduke cannot attempt any serious operations from that quarter till the month of April; but the war in Catalonia will continue throughout the winter, and if we do not put ourselves in a position to attack the enemy, the enemy will enter Aragon, and even Castile, before Christmas with twenty thousand men. The Archduke has already with him seven thousand Englishmen as well as three thousand Neapolitan and Spanish deserters, and he can count upon twelve thousand Catalonians. If we content ourselves with merely assuming a defensive attitude, all these forces will come down upon us, and as we have not a single town on the Catalonian frontier that can be garrisoned, the Archduke will soon oblige our troops to retreat to Madrid, a city which can be forced to surrender, through famine, in eight days."

Madame des Ursins goes on to urge that troops should be sent from France without delay, both in the interest of Philip V. and of Louis XIV.

Early in 1706 Philip V. endeavoured to carry out the plan suggested by Madame des Ursins in her letter to M. de Torcy. He marched with Marshal Tessé to Barcelona and besieged it on the land side, while the Count of Toulouse, who commanded the French ships of war, blockaded the harbour. The place had almost succumbed when the English fleet unexpectedly appeared, and Barcelona was relieved. Philip hastily broke up the siege and fled, "abandoning his heavy artillery and stores, and consigning the sick and wounded to the humanity of the enemy." In the morning, we are told, the sky was darkened by a total eclipse of the sun, and as the sun was the emblem of the House of Bourbon, this circumstance was considered by many as a sure omen of the downfall of that family. There is a curious medal at the British Museum, struck by the Allies to commemorate their success at Barcelona. Philip V. is represented on horseback flying from the field of action and hurling his crown to the ground, whilst a winged figure of "Victory" eclipses the sun with a shield bearing the arms of Austria.

Madame des Ursins writes to Madame de Maintenon : " The lamentable news has reached us that the siege [of Barcelona] is raised, and that the King, being unable to effect his retreat through Aragon, has been forced to retire into France by way of Roussillon.

"It is melancholy to think that our unhappy Sovereign is retreating with troops who have been defeated, who are weary and dejected, and who cannot even command the necessaries of life. And we cannot forget that they are traversing that infamous Catalonia, where they are exposed at every turn to be harassed by ambushed ruffians. . . . Still, though we fully recognise the crushing blow we have received, I can assure you, Madame, that our courage does not waver, and that no plan of action will be adopted until it has received the most mature consideration."

She writes again (April 16-18, 1706): "Alas! Madame, what sad news awaits you from Estramadura! We have just lost Alcantara, and with it ten battalions whom the enemy have made prisoners of war. We knew that the place could not hold out for long as it is not a stronghold, but we hoped that the garrison would, at least, have been saved. It is evident, however, that Marshal Berwick was unable to prevent this disaster, since his zeal for the service is equal to his skill and knowledge. I know not what would become of us if our enemies were capable of taking every advantage of their success, for in this country there is not a single place than can be considered secure for two days together. . . . The Queen, plunged as she is in the midst of trials that might well confound the understanding of the most experienced head and daunt the courage of the stoutest heart, shows no sign of weakness, but bears with patient resignation whatever it may be the will of God to send her. This conduct affords me much consolation.

"It often happens, I find, Madame, that when we fancy all is lost some happy turn of events changes the aspect of our affairs. I now live in this hope; though I derive it, I believe, rather from my cheerful temperament than from my sober reason; being at all times more ready to believe in the coming of happy events than to anticipate misfortunes."

Whilst the cause of Philip V. was suffering

in Spain it fared no better in the Netherlands. On May 23, 1706, the great battle of Ramillies was fought, when Marlborough completely defeated Villeroy. This battle was "as decisive for the Netherlands as Blenheim had been for Bavaria. The Allies took Brussels and Malines, Ghent and Bruges, and in them proclaimed Charles III. King of Spain and Overlord of the Netherlands; Antwerp and Oudenarde threw open their gates, and Brabant took oath to the Austro-Spanish King. So strong was the feeling in favour of Charles, that Louis XIV. did not venture, as heretofore, to make war in the name of the King of Spain." The campaign in Italy had been equally disastrous for French and Spanish interests. The Austrians now "triumphed from Naples to the Alps . . . and the Pope was compelled to recognise Charles III. as King of Spain." *

The Princess des Ursins writes to Madame de Maintenon on June 16: "Two days ago I put a letter, which I had the honour of writing to you, into the hands of the Duc de Noailles.

* See Kitchen's "History of France."

In it I acquainted you with the condition of our affairs at that time and described our uncertainty as to the wisest course of action for the Queen to adopt. Marshal Berwick has now solved the question, for he has informed us that no doubt can be entertained as to the movements of the enemy. They are marching straight for Madrid, and since it is impossible to defend the towns through which they must pass, it is absolutely necessary for the Queen to quit Madrid, and that without loss of time. . . . The grandees do all in their power to persuade their Majesties to remain quietly in their capital and to submit to whatever conditions the enemy may choose to impose; but these counsels find no favour. The King and Queen consider that neither their honour nor their safety would be secured by such a course. . . . In this painful state of affairs, those of us who are French might well feel special alarm, but we entertain no such feeling: we do our duty and trust in God for His help."

CHAPTER VII

A ROYAL FUGITIVE

THE Duke of Berwick had been forced to retreat before the victorious army of the enemy, and, knowing that it was impossible for him to defend Madrid with his small band of 8000 men, he had advised the removal of the Court to Burgos. It was high time for this, for scarcely had Philip quitted his capital "than the light troops of Galway and Das Minas appeared in sight and, on the 28th day of June, those chiefs, at the head of 20,000 men, made a triumphant entry into Madrid."

Philip joined his army, whilst the Queen, accompanied by Madame des Ursins and a few attendants, made her retreat northwards. They were escorted by a French regiment under the command of the Chevalier Bragelonne. From

Berlanga, where they halted to take rest, Madame des Ursins writes to Madame de Maintenon (June 24, 1706): "We were forced to quit Madrid, and as it was deemed expedient to conceal our intentions up to the last moment, we came away without any proper provision being made for the journey. The Queen had not even a bed to sleep on during the first few nights.

"It has been decided that the Queen shall go to Burgos. The Count de Santestevan, Grand Steward of her household, the Marquis de Castel Rodrigue, her Chief Equerry, and the Duke de Popoli, one of the four captains of the King's Guard, were of opinion that she should go to Pampeluna, where she would be in greater safety and less exposed to the risk of having again to retreat before the enemy. But the King, the French Ambassador, and the Duke de Berwick preferred Burgos, because it is a city of Castile, and the King desires to establish his Councils there, hoping by this means to keep the people from revolt. . . . The day after to-morrow the Queen must proceed to Aranda de Douero which is only twelve leagues from Segovia. It is to be hoped that the enemy's reinforcements, now on board the English fleet, may not land at Bilbao, because in that case our retreat would be completely cut off. The enemy would reach Vittoria before the Queen could get there, and the Miquelets, who have stirred up the rebellion in Aragon, would effectually bar our retreat in that direction. . . .

"The Queen's retinue is sadly reduced. It consists only of myself, one lady-in-waiting, and one maid. Our total want of funds is the cause of this. The Queen had nominated two more ladies of the Court to accompany her, but when they learnt of their nomination, they each demanded payment of a hundred pistoles that were due to them. As this demand could not be complied with . . . these ladies remained behind. Our travelling expenses are heavy in spite of the small number of the Queen's attendants, for we are obliged to carry everything we require along with us. The cost each day amounts to nearly a hundred pistoles. The money for this purpose has been obtained mostly on credit—a source which must soon fail us, and when that happens we may find ourselves in an awkward position.

"The King has written to the Queen to propose their sending the crown jewels to France in order that they may be sold or mortgaged. Her Majesty has at once consented, and they will be carried to France by the same courier who bears this letter. Among the gems there is the famous pearl entitled the 'Pelegrina' and also the diamond called by the Spaniards the 'Estanqué' (clear pool). The Queen has added to the store all her own personal ornaments. Vazet, an old retainer of the King's, takes charge of the treasure. He will be accompanied by an officer (a foster-brother of the Duc de Berri) who has been highly recommended to me by Mons. de Bragelonne . . . I am addressing the packet to Mons. de Labourdonnay, Governor of Bordeaux, who is now staying at Bayonne."

Both the pearl and diamond alluded to are mentioned in a letter, written by Madame d'Aulnoy in 1680, describing the public entry into Madrid of Charles II.'s bride. "She wore," says the writer, "a hat and feathers on which was displayed the pearl called the Peregrina, which is as large as a small pear and is of inestimable value. Upon her finger was the great diamond belonging to the King which is said to be the most beautiful in Europe."

Leaving Berlanga the travellers proceeded on their journey towards Burgos. Their route lay through "a dreary, lifeless, treeless, waterless country," where they were exposed to the burning rays of a July sun. Madame des Ursins writes from Lerma (July 4, 1706): "The Queen reached this place yesterday. The heat is unusually great, even for this country, and such as is never experienced in France. Her Majesty was obliged to make a halt here in order that the horses might have rest, for to-morrow they must take us to Burgos. The Court and the Councils will be established in that city until the time comes when the King may return to Madrid.

"We have travelled by a much longer route than we should naturally have taken, in order to avoid the enemies' troops. This measure was deemed necessary by the Duke de Popoli and others who are charged with the safe conduct of the Queen. . . . But when we learnt there was no cause for alarm in these districts, we retraced our steps so that we might not approach the borders of Navarre. Had we advanced towards that province the enemy would have supposed that the Queen was retreating to France, and that the King's intention was to join her there and to abandon Spain to the Archduke. Our countermarch has cost us four long days' journey, but it was necessary in order to inspire the troops with confidence, and to convince the loyal subjects that their Majesties will defend them to the last. The inhabitants of the country through which we have passed appear to be warmly attached to Philip V., but unfortunately for him Castile is the poorest portion of Spain, and we must remember that this nation is no longer what it once was. Towns of even considerable size have not sufficient courage to refuse a summons to surrender, however insignificant the enemy's force may be.

". . . The Queen's health continues good in spite of all the trials she has had to undergo. Her courage could hardly be put to a severer test, nor could she, I think, ever merit more praise for her resignation to the will of God than she merits now." "(Burgos, July 7.) I am finishing this letter at Burgos, where the Queen arrived the evening before last, and where she was greeted by the acclamations of the inhabitants. At night they collected beneath her windows, and serenaded her with loyal choruses celebrating the praises of herself and the King. When the music ceased the Queen stepped on to the balcony and cried 'Viva los Castellanos!' These words created transports of delight and enthusiasm."

The travellers had suffered many privations during their journey from Madrid to Burgos. The Queen wrote to Madame de Maintenon the morning after her arrival (July 6): "After a journey of eighteen days I arrived at Burgos yesterday evening, much fatigued with rising before daybreak, overpowered with the heat, almost stifled with the dust, and having rested only in the most wretched and ruinous hovels. We hoped on arriving here to be more comfortably lodged, but have hitherto been greatly disappointed. We shall not complain, however, in spite of these hardships, if the King can but prevail over his enemies. Unhappily, scarcely a day passes without bringing us the news of some fresh disaster."*

Madame de Maintenon, in her letters to the Princess des Ursins, expresses heartfelt sorrow for the trials of the young King and Queen and for those of her friend. "How terrible it is," she exclaims, "to think of the Queen, at the age of eighteen, deprived of her throne and a wanderer, begging a night's shelter from her subjects! . . . The Duchess of Burgundy† read me your letter yesterday, and we both shed many tears over it." And again she writes: "*Your* cause is betrayed by the Spaniards,

* See " Mémoires de Noailles."
† Sister to the Queen of Spain.

whilst *our* cause is abandoned by the Flemish. Surely we must have incurred the wrath of the Almighty!"

Madame des Ursins, ever cheerful under circumstances the most untoward, writes to Madame de Maintenon from Burgos (July 13, 1706): "I must give you some amusement, dear Madame, by a description of my apartments. They consist of a single room of about twelve or thirteen feet square. A large window, facing south, occupies nearly the whole of one wall. This window is open and we are unable to close it. A small door leads into the Queen's chamber, and a second door, yet smaller, leads into a winding passage. I dare not explore this passage, for although there are lamps hung here and there which shed some light, it is so illpaved that I might stumble and break my neck. I cannot describe the walls as *white*, for they are blackened with dirt. The furniture consists of my small travelling bed, a camp-stool, and a deal table. At this table I alternately arrange my toilet, write my letters, and eat my bread and fruit. As to appliances for cooking, there are none, and perhaps if there were, we should have no money to spend on dainties. Her Majesty only laughs at all this, and I laugh also." The house in which the Queen was lodged was the Casa del Cordón, the mansion of the Constable of Castile, a grand structure, with its towers, sculptured arms, and the symbolic *rope* over the portal. Madame des Ursins' description is evidence of the dire poverty that affected even the nobles at this period.

Many members of the Court now followed the Queen to Burgos. Madame de Maintenon, in one of her letters to the Princess des Ursins, had expressed her concern at the discomforts which these must suffer in the poor accommodation at Burgos. To this the Princess responds: "Pray do not trouble yourself to feel pity for the ladies and gentlemen who have followed the Queen here. . . . You are probably sympathising with those who, for the most part, care little whether Charles III. or Philip V. is their master, and who are cautiously waiting to declare their sentiments until they see which side is likely to be victorious. If you could see and hear all that we see and hear you would perceive how necessary it is for us to be on our guard and to watch vigilantly the conduct of these persons, so that we may know in time how we should act. . . . And now Madame," she concludes, "I must leave off writing, though much against my will, for I am always happy and at ease whilst conversing with you. It seems as if I were once more by your side in that favoured spot where there is perfect shelter alike from the winds of heaven and from the treachery of men." Again Madame des Ursins writes (Burgos, August 12): "The provinces continue to levy troops for their defence. Even the poorest localities are eager to contribute their share, and more than their share, of men and money. The day before yesterday a curé brought the Queen 120 pistoles.* His whole village contains but 120 people, all of whom are very poor. He told her Majesty that his flock were ashamed

* The Spanish pistole, or doubloon, was at that time worth £3 6s. 5½d.

DOORWAY OF THE HOUSE OF THE CORDÓN, BURGOS

to send her so little, but they wished her to consider that their purse contained 120 hearts that would remain faithful to the King's cause until death. The good man wept as he spoke, and we wept with him."

Even in Madrid, where the Archduke's army had now its headquarters, the common people remained faithful to Philip. When Charles was proclaimed King by his generals, no shout of applause had greeted the announcement; "a mournful silence reigned on every side."

Toledo declared for Charles. But this was not brought about by the inclinations of the inhabitants generally, but by the influence of those in authority. The Queen-Dowager of Spain, an Austrian princess, resided in that city. She had, in her heart, always wished success to her nephew the Archduke, although outwardly professing attachment to Philip V. and his Queen. She had a powerful ally in Cardinal Portocarero, who had recently abandoned the Bourbon cause and joined the party of the Archduke. No sooner did a squadron of the enemies' horse appear before the walls of Toledo than the gates were thrown open for their reception. The Queen-Dowager evinced her joy in an unusual way; for, casting aside her mourning garments, which Spanish widows were condemned to wear for the remainder of their lives, she put on festival attire and, attended by all her household, welcomed the conquerors. The Cardinal, after performing a solemn "Te Deum" in the cathedral, blessed the Austrian standards in person; and at night, the archiepiscopal palace blazed with a joyful illumination and spread forth a costly banquet in honour of the day.

Saragossa revolted without even seeing the enemy, and "the Governor of Carthagena betrayed his trust and surrendered to the Allies the best arsenal and the best ships which Spain possessed."

The Princess des Ursins writes to Madame de Maintenon from Burgos (September 23, 1706): "I sincerely wish, dear Madame, that I could relieve your anxiety by giving you better news of our unhappy Spain, but that is out of my power. It is true that the Archduke will probably return to Valencia, and that he leaves Castile undefended on that side; but, in the meantime, five or six thousand Portuguese, who had invested Salamanca, have taken the city by storm. They burnt down several churches ... and afterwards seized upon the monks of St. Jerome, whose fidelity to their legitimate Sovereign was well known, and massacred them all. This barbarous deed has pierced me to the heart, and the Queen, who has just learnt the terrible news, is deeply affected."

Madame des Ursins, in the midst of such trials as these, could yet cheer and comfort Madame de Maintenon in *her* trials. The French armies were suffering defeat after defeat in Italy. After expressing her sympathy and concern, she observes: "but we may well hope that the Almighty, who has witnessed the resignation of our two kings to the divine decrees, will one day reward their virtues and display His own power by some signal act in our favour. Let us, then, keep up our courage, dear Madame, and let us use all the means put in our power to mitigate the dire evils of France and Spain."

Madame des Ursins' actions during this unhappy period did not belie her words. By indefatigable exertions and wisely conceived plans she obtained large gifts of money from the province of Burgos and from the cities of Andalusia. With this timely aid the troops were paid, clothes and provisions were provided, and the danger of desertion was warded off. Philip, delighted with this unexpected help, wrote to Madame des Ursins to express his gratitude for the great service she had rendered his cause.

From this time forward the face of affairs began to change in favour of Philip. The Castilians had hitherto remained strangely inactive. They had allowed the enemy to sweep across their country, conquering city after city, and at last to enter their very capital itself. But now when resistance seemed to be well-nigh hopeless "the national spirit awoke fierce, proud, and unconquerable." The Castilians threw off their lethargy and rallied round their young King with generous devotion. Religious enthusiasm was mingled with their feelings of loyalty. For in the eyes of the old Catholics of Castile a king has always borne a peculiarly sacred character; so sacred, indeed, that they apply to him the same titles which they apply to the Deity. The attempt, therefore, of the enemy to wrest the crown from Philip appeared to them an act of sacrilege, and as such they felt bound to oppose it to the uttermost.

The Allied Powers supposed that all the territory they had conquered would remain in the hands of the Archduke, but they now saw their mistake. "There is no country in Europe," says Macaulay, "which is so easy to overrun as Spain. There is no country in Europe which is more difficult to conquer. . . . War in Spain has, from the days of the Romans, had a character of its own: it is a fire which cannot be raked out; it burns fiercely under the embers; and long after it has, to all seeming, been extinguished, bursts forth more violently than ever." On all sides the country was rising up in arms against the invaders. "Every peasant procured a firelock or a pike; the Allies were masters only of the ground on which they trod." To add to their difficulties the Allies had endless causes of division in their own camp, where too many nationalities were represented. It was no easy task to maintain concord amongst the English, the Dutch, the Austrians, the Spaniards of Aragon and Catalonia, and their hereditary enemies the Portuguese. But the Archduke Charles was not the leader even to attempt it. There is a portrait of him at the British Museum, taken soon after he was proclaimed King of Spain by the Allies. He bears the title of Charles III. and is represented with the crown by his side and all the other emblems of regal dignity. The face is that of a young man of about two-and-twenty. The features are heavy, and the protruding under-lip denotes self-will and obstinacy; qualities of which his English Allies had bitter experience. The Archduke usually followed his own inclinations, or turned for advice to his favourite German officers, who, had "great arrogance and no military knowledge," and who "were alternately bursting with presumption or benumbed with fear." When the presence of Charles was sorely needed by his party in Madrid, and the English generals were urging him to hasten to that city, he was wasting his time in Catalonia. He told General Stanhope that this delay was unavoidable, as his equipage was not ready to enter the capital with becoming state. "Sir," replied the General, "our William the Third entered London in a hackney coach with a cloak-bag behind it, and was made King not many weeks after."[*] When, at last, the day arrived which Charles had fixed upon for his triumphal entry into Madrid, and when all his preparations were complete, his opportunity was lost. By that time his troops had been forced to evacuate the capital, and they were retreating with all speed to Aragon, whilst Philip's troops were entering the city amidst the joyful acclamations of the inhabitants. "Never was greater joy evinced," writes Madame des Ursins, "nor was there

[*] Lord Mahon.

ever perhaps a more striking example given of devotion to a Sovereign. . . . The people pillaged the houses of those who had been most ardent in the cause of the Archduke. . . . But not one of the men who perpetrated the deed would touch the spoil. They carried all the property they had laid hands upon into the public squares, and burnt it, declaring that they had not pillaged in order to enrich themselves, but in order to punish traitors."

"At Toledo the people rose in insurrection against Portocarero and the Queen-Dowager, tore down the Austrian standard, which the latter had hoisted on her palace, placed guards at her door, and treated her as a prisoner of state." *

On the 4th of October Philip V. returned to his capital, and soon afterwards the Queen, accompanied by Madame des Ursins, quitted Burgos, and commenced her journey southwards. She halted at a place called Cabaron near Burgos, and alighted at a house which is now No. 2 in the Calla del Rio. Over the door of this house

* Lord Mahon.

there is a tablet of stone bearing the arms of Spain and Savoy, and having an inscription to the following effect: "The Queen, our Lady Doña Louisa Gabriela of Savoy, honoured this house by staying in it on the 17th October, 1706." Philip came to Segovia to meet his wife. The royal couple had not seen each other since their sorrowful parting in Madrid four months before. "It is impossible to describe their joy in meeting again," writes Madame des Ursins. "When the State carriages appeared the Queen ran out into the street to meet the King before he had time to alight. Rain was falling in torrents and she was wet to the skin, but she had gained the pleasure of embracing him a moment earlier than she could have done had she awaited his arrival in the hall; that was a sufficient reward for her." They reached Madrid on October 27. Before making their entry into the capital, the King and Queen, accompanied by their Court, attended high Mass at the Church of the Virgin of Atocha, where special homage is paid on occasions of importance. The image of the Virgin is of such antiquity that it is blackened with age, but it is always sumptuously attired, having for its special perquisite the wedding dresses of the Queens of Spain.

"The progress of their Catholic Majesties through the city," writes Madame des Ursins, "took nearly three hours, so much did the throng of people who pressed round the carriage impede its course. These shouted and cheered without ceasing the whole way."

Philip V. showed forbearance in his treatment of those who had espoused the cause of the Archduke. The "Cardinal Portocarero was forgiven in memory of his past services, and the Queen-Dowager was respectfully escorted out of Spain."

The Duke of Berwick in his "Memoirs" describes the campaign of 1706 as "one of the most singular on record from its rapid changes of fortune." "Had the enemy," he remarks, "known how to profit by their success and pushed their point, the Archduke must have been King." But the "glaring faults of their generals, together with the unparalleled fidelity of the Castilians, changed the course of events." The enemy was driven back into Valencia, and the number of prisoners taken amounted to ten thousand.

CHAPTER VIII

A NEW HOPE

THE scattered members of the Court of Madrid were now rapidly returning to the capital. A great many ladies-in-waiting had refused, as we have seen, to follow the Queen to Burgos, and their near relations had espoused the cause of the Archduke. Here, then, was an opportunity for effecting some reduction in the Queen's household such as had already been effected in the King's household. The number of ladies at the Court had at all times been far too large and was the cause of an extravagant expenditure. At the suggestion of the Camarera-Mayor Philip now dismissed no fewer than three hundred maids of honour!

"The King of Spain," writes Madame des Ursins, "who has barely sufficient money to pay his troops, thinks it advisable to retrench his expenditure in every possible way. He considers that the ladies-in-waiting are not as indispensable to the Crown as are the means for the maintenance of its soldiers. Monsieur l'Ambassadeur is of the same opinion. His Majesty, has, therefore, informed most of the ladies [of the Court] that he is obliged, to his great regret, to request them not to return for the present to the Queen's service. This proceeding will doubtless bring upon me personally a great deal of enmity. Those who are reasonable, however, are well aware that we must avoid all expenditure which is not absolutely necessary. The most pressing question is how to repulse the invaders. All else in comparison is a mere trifle."

Madame des Ursins' personal enemies were already sufficiently numerous, and they were ever active in fabricating reports to her disadvantage. Much licence of speech prevailed at the beginning of the eighteenth century, as is shown by the memoirs of that day. Calumnies were circulated concerning all conspicuous persons. The excellent Amelot was not spared any more than was Madame des Ursins. Philip V. was so much annoyed by the malicious reports regarding affairs in Spain which found their way across the border, that he wrote to his grandfather urging him to put a stop to them. The answer of Louis XIV. is remarkable, coming as it does from such a quarter: "I wish," he writes, "that I could put an end to the kind of talk of which your Majesty complains; but it is impossible to deprive the public of liberty of speech. The public has enjoyed this right at all times and in all countries, and more especially in France. We must endeavour, for our part, to act in such a manner as to afford occasion for approving comments only."*

Madame des Ursins, it is needless to say, was too sensible to suppose that any arbitrary action in such a case could be of service. The ultra-French faction, she knew, must always be opposed to her more liberal policy, and she had long borne their enmity with courage and

* "Mémoires de Noailles."

dignity. To her intimate friends alone she occasionally opened her heart on this subject. Writing this same year (1706) to Marshal Villeroi, she alludes to the trials of her position, and then proceeds to speak of their common friend Madame de Maintenon: "It is from this staunch and generous friend," she remarks, "that I derive my chief consolation. What should I do without her goodness?—I, who am persecuted more than ever by my enemies in France, and subjected in Madrid to ill-will and envy, because my sole aim is to further the true interests of the two Kings!"

In a letter to Madame de Maintenon, dated December 20, she points out, half playfully, how busy the tongue of calumny has been with both herself and her correspondent. "I received two letters some time ago," she writes, "which I ought to have communicated to you ere this. The first letter informed me that you were betraying the interests of France by means of a secret correspondence with Queen Anne; and that the Queen knew you to be the best friend the Prince of Orange ever possessed!

The second letter disclosed the fact that you were sending large sums of money to the Emperor to enable him to maintain his troops. For Heaven's sake, Madame, cure yourself of that dangerous practice of self-seeking which leads you to commit such crimes! You will reply, perhaps, that I should do well to follow my own salutary advice, and should forthwith abandon my practice of selling the high offices of this country for my own profit." Here Madame des Ursins changes her tone of irony to one of indignation. "Such," she exclaims, "is the idle gossip of the world, where men and women are for ever slandering each other!"

Responding to some observations of her friend, she remarks: "I entirely agree with you, Madame, that there is as much ability as there is virtue in upright conduct. Duplicity and falsehood are discovered sooner or later, and more advantages are to be gained than lost by just dealing, which commands the respect of all honest men, not to speak of the peace of mind which results from a desire to act openly and to deceive no one."

The recent Austrian occupation of Madrid had left behind it much bitterness of feeling, and revived many animosities. Madame des Ursins writes to her friend: "You ask me if I am able to retain my usual tranquillity in the midst of so many causes for disquietude. I will answer your question by telling you frankly that I do at times experience agitation, especially on hearing suddenly some painful piece of news. At such moments I feel almost ready to faint. . . . But the weakness is quickly overcome, and I am myself again. I cheer my mind with the thought that affairs may change for the better. I turn the medal and look on the reverse side, whence I derive cause for hope. I wish, Madame, that you could do the same, and that your own temperament were your best friend, as mine has ever been to me. . . . For my part, I owe to the Almighty, among countless other blessings, a cheerful disposition which prompts me to despair of nothing. Indeed, I am fully persuaded that by courage, perseverance, and firmness the direst difficulties may be overcome, provided the motive for action be the welfare of the public." Well might Madame de Maintenon respond: "Your letters communicate your very self in the most inspiring manner. They bring before me that courage which can endure all things without wavering, and that sunny nature which can regard nothing with melancholy or bitterness."

It seems remarkable that Madame des Ursins could write with such freedom at a time when letters were often tampered with by the emissaries of Government. The Duchess of Orleans (mother of the Regent), complains that her letters from Germany were frequently opened by the French officials, who passed them on to her with their seals broken, not even taking the trouble to fasten them up again. But Madame des Ursins had this advantage over the Duchess, that her letters were conveyed to Versailles by the French Ambassador Amelot's special couriers, and that she and Amelot were at all times fast friends. It is at any rate certain that the contents of the private letters of Madame de Maintenon and the Princess des Ursins were not publicly known, since, had they been known, the ladies' opinions of the Kings of France and of Spain, and of all the leading statesmen of the day, would have been circulated with avidity, and must have transpired in the memoirs of that period.

The character of the young King of Spain had gained some strength from the trials to which he had been exposed. Madame des Ursins writes to her friend (December 6, 1706) : " The King displays an interest in the affairs of State and a steadiness of application to business that is quite remarkable. He is no longer the same being who had to be urged to exert himself and to act with authority. He is now fully conscious that he possesses authority, and the consciousness affords him pleasure. He desires to understand all that goes on, and forms his opinion with sense and judgment. . . . He decides boldly, and, what is of still more importance, his decisions are marked by justice, generosity, and firmness. I leave you to judge, Madame,' she continues, " how rejoiced I must be at this change—I, who have so long and so ardently desired it." Madame de Maintenon responds: "Nothing is more astonishing than the sudden alteration in the King [of Spain]! It is certainly a miracle. *Our* King is greatly pleased and hopes there may be no relapse." These last words show in what estimation Louis XIV. held his grandson. In fact, Madame des Ursins had, in her enthusiasm, given Philip credit for more than was his due. "If the King inspired respect and fear," remarks François Combes, "it was through Madame des Ursins that he did so. She alone, in spite of her eulogium on his change of character, kept him up to a high standard of principle and of action."

At the commencement of the year 1707 a source of satisfaction arose for those who favoured the Bourbon dynasty—namely, the hope of an heir to the throne; a hope which Spain's reigning family had not known for more than forty years. The news was publicly announced on January 29, and on the following day Madame des Ursins writes to Madame de Maintenon: "The transports of joy with which the news was received can hardly be described. The people thronged the streets [round the palace] singing and shouting as if they were mad."

It was customary for the Queens of Spain, under such circumstances, to repair in solemn procession to the Church of the Virgin of Atocha in order to pay their homage at her shrine. "The important function," writes Madame des Ursins, "took place last Saturday. The Queen was borne in a sedan-chair; I followed in another; next came the equipages of the ladies of honour; and then those of the gentlemen of her Majesty's household." Barriers had been erected all along the route to keep off the pressure of the crowd. "These barriers," continues Madame des Ursins, "extended the whole way from the palace to the Church of Atocha. They were lined with soldiers under arms, and at intervals stood trumpeters and hautboy-players. The streets were gaily decorated. Rich tapestries of various colours hung from the balconies and window ledges. In some places pictures and mirrors were suspended in front of draperies of crimson silk, while beneath them glittered articles of silver plate. Here and there fountains appeared surrounded by allegorical figures and decorated with flowers and green tracery. A throng of people accompanied the procession, singing and shouting their praises of the King and Queen. Some wept for joy and called upon Heaven to grant the royal couple fifty children, who should live for ever; others laughed aloud. . . . The grandees walked on either side of her Majesty's sedan-chair. Some who are old or infirm could hardly drag themselves along. The Queen graciously desired these to leave her, but this they could not bring themselves to do, so they accompanied her right into the Chapel of the Virgin. The King, who had already arrived there attended by the chief officers of his household, stood on the steps of the church to receive the Queen, and with ready gallantry opened the door of her sedan-chair. Their Majesties returned to the palace (after the service was over) in the same manner, and although the function lasted for four hours, the Queen has not suffered from over-fatigue."

Preparations were now commenced to welcome a Prince of Asturias. Apartments in the palace were assigned to his future use, the furniture and decorations for which were ordered to be sent from Paris. Madame des Ursins gives minute directions in her letters as to the carrying out of these orders, urging at the same time the necessity for economy. She specifies the amount of yellow silk to be used for covering the chairs, and remarks that she will arrange for some of the pictures in the royal collection to be hung on the walls of the apartments to obviate the necessity of having new tapestry hangings. She desires that the lace upon the bed linen should be narrow. "Lavish expenditure," she remarks, "would indeed be out of place at a time when the King of Spain is resolutely denying himself every luxury. . . . People hold widely different views," she continues to her friend, "as to what constitutes true dignity in this world, but I am happy to know that we both agree in thinking that a Prince of Asturias is equally worthy of our homage whether he lies in a plain cot or in one bedizened with gold."

Money was indeed needed at this period to maintain the army. The enemy had, it is true, been driven from Madrid, but they occupied strong positions in Valencia, Aragon, and Catalonia, and might at any moment return as victors to the capital. The French contingent of the forces received so little support from home that the Spanish Government had to advance money for its maintenance as well as for that of its own troops. Madame des Ursins writes to Madame de Maintenon: "The French military secretary, Monsieur Méliaud, has received only one month's pay for the French soldiers from Monsieur de Chamillart, out of six that are due to them. . . . Marshal Berwick knows not how to act. His troops must either desert or they must pillage Castile, a choice of evils equally disastrous to our cause."

CHAPTER IX

TIDINGS OF VICTORY

In the early part of 1706 Madame des Ursins had endeavoured to obtain a loan from the clergy towards the expenses of the war. Her project failed owing to the determined opposition of Cardinal Portocarero, who had secretly joined the Archduke's party. The Cardinal was, moreover, encouraged in his opposition by the Pope. François Combe, in his " Essai sur la Princesse des Ursins," has pointed out the curious attitude assumed by the Pope at this period. The War of the Spanish Succession was, he reminds us, in many respects a religious war, in which the old Catholic interest was represented by the two Bourbon Kings, and the Protestant by the Archduke Charles. For although Charles was himself a Catholic, his powerful supporters were all Protestants, a circumstance which was ridiculed in a satirical medal of the day. It bears the head of the Archduke encircled by the words, "Charles III., by the grace of the Heretics the Catholic King." Parties being thus divided, it would seem natural for the Pope to have done all in his power to aid the cause of Philip V., but, on the contrary, he acted continually as his opponent. It is true Clement IX. had recognised the Bourbon succession, but he secretly favoured the cause of the Allies because they advocated the dismemberment of the Spanish dominions, and he ardently desired to see the Kings of Spain forced to give up the kingdom of Naples.

In the autumn of 1706 Madame des Ursins renewed her efforts to obtain a loan from the Spanish clergy for the expenses of the war, and this time her efforts were crowned with success. M. Geffroy tells us that she obtained a sum of no less than four million dollars (equal to £800,000). By this means the wants of the army were supplied, and the Duke of Berwick found himself in a position to make head against the enemy.

Madame des Ursins writes to Madame de Maintenon on April 17, 1707: "We are on the eve of some decisive action, and we have reason to hope it may be in our favour. The two opposing armies are now only four leagues apart. All our officers, whether Spanish or French, are confident of victory, and declare openly that unless our general gives battle they shall be driven to despair. But we may be sure that Marshal Berwick will do his duty, and in the meantime let us pray the Almighty to enable him to come to a wise decision."

On April 25, just a week after the above letter was written, the great battle of Almanza was fought. The Duke of Berwick commanded the French and Spanish forces, and the Earl of Galway, the English, Dutch, and Portuguese. Galway, known in France as the Marquis de Ruvigny, was a Huguenot who had fled to England after the Revocation of the Edict of Nantes. In recognition of his military services he had been created an Irish peer. Thus, by a curious coincidence the French and Spanish armies were commanded by an Englishman, and the English army by a Frenchman. No Spanish troops fought this day in the ranks of the Allies, as the Archduke at this critical moment had withdrawn his Spanish contingent and retired with it into Catalonia.

The battle, which raged fiercely for some time, resulted in a victory for Philip V. "The victory was most complete," writes Lord Mahon; "all the baggage and artillery was taken, together with one hundred and twenty standards bearing the arms of almost every nation leagued against France and Spain, besides those of the insurgent provinces of Valencia, Aragon, and Catalonia. . . . The Allies left above four thousand men dead upon the field, and twice as many prisoners. . . . So large was the booty that for some days after the battle a horse might be purchased in the camp of Berwick for one dollar, a coat for fifteen French pence, and a musket for five."

The news of the great victory was received at Madrid with transports of joy—a joy that

DUKE OF BERWICK, GENERALISSIMO OF THE FORCES IN SPAIN

was soon afterwards shared by the Court of Versailles. Madame des Ursins writes to Madame de Maintenon: "Let us rejoice together, and let us render thanks to God who has enabled us to gain such a victory over our foes! What happiness the news will afford the King and all the royal family; and what consolation it will bring to you, Madame! I will not attempt to describe what *my* feelings are on the occasion; you can well imagine them by your own."

"You judged rightly," responds her friend, "of what the joy of the King and the royal family would be. I must describe to you the way in which the news reached us. You know Marly and will remember my private apartments. The King was in my small room. I had just sat down to my supper in the antechamber, when I heard an officer calling loudly at the King's door to announce Monsieur de Chamillart. 'How is this?' exclaimed the King, for in the ordinary course of things a Minister is not permitted an audience at such a time. I threw down my napkin and turned to

Monsieur de Chamillart in much agitation. "It is good news," said he, and immediately entered the King's room, followed by Monsieur de Silly. You may well believe, madame, that I followed also. I soon learnt from the King of the defeat of our enemies, and returned to my supper in the most happy frame of mind. Soon afterwards Monsieur le Dauphin came to see the King, and next the Duke of Burgundy, who appeared with a billiard cue in his hand. . . . Madame de Dangeau quitted the supper table in order to write to her husband, who is in Paris, and our invalid Madame d'Heudicourt likewise quitted the supper table in order to seek quiet in my chamber."

Madame des Ursins was delighted with the foregoing account. Her vivid imagination at once pictured the whole scene, and she gave *back* to Madame de Maintenon a reflex of her story in the following letter. "All that you relate, Madame, from the appearance of the officer who announced the arrival of Monsieur de Chamillart, . . . when you were seated quietly at supper in your antechamber, until the moment when his Majesty proclaimed the great news, is so lifelike that I begin to think I must have been present myself and seen you throw down your napkin and hurry into the adjoining room to hear what was being told. I can see Madame de Dangeau flying from the supper table to write to her husband, Madame d'Heudicourt walking about as if her limbs were young and strong, hardly knowing what she was doing, and Monsieur de Marson, in spite of his gout, jumping on to a chair with as much agility as if he had been a tight-rope dancer, to see what was going forward. As for Monseigneur the Duke of Burgundy, who, we know, is somewhat absent-minded, I wonder that, in the first transports of his joy, he did not mistake a lady's head for a billiard ball, and give her a blow with the cue which he carried in his hand!"

Madame de Maintenon responds to her friend: "You have certainly pictured the whole scene far better than I who witnessed it."

When the tidings of the great defeat reached the Archduke and his Court at Barcelona, the effect produced was curious. The jealousy and dislike of the English was so strong amongst Charles's German followers that at first "feelings of gratified pique rose uppermost." When, however, the magnitude of their own loss was comprehended, " the Germans were stunned and fell into a profound lethargy." *

Meanwhile the victorious army marched steadily forward, and within a month of the battle of Almanza, both the provinces of Valencia and Aragon were subdued. Berwick treated the vanquished with stern severity. In the case of the town of Xativa the carnage was terrible, but that General states distinctly in his " Memoirs " that the inhabitants persistently refused all offers of capitulation.

Alluding to the taking of Xativa, Madame des Ursins writes: "Although there never were people more deserving of their punishment, and although that punishment may serve as a warning to others who are equally violent in their opposition to their Sovereign, still the affair strikes one with horror. War brings

* Lord Mahon.

many a crime in its train, and I cannot conceive how kings who carry on unjust wars can expect that the Almighty will ever forgive them."

Although Berwick acted sternly towards the vanquished, he was a man of strict integrity and did not spare himself when occasion required. After the battle of Almanza he was created Duke of Liria and a grandee of Spain, dignities which he afterwards transferred to his second son. "In the year 1719," writes Lord Mahon, "this son found himself a general officer in the Spanish army, and opposed to his father, who commanded the French, the two nations being then at war. With his true and characteristic sense of honour, however, Berwick wrote an earnest letter to Liria, exhorting him to do his duty against himself."

Upon the subjection of Valencia and Aragon, the Spanish Government issued a decree abolishing the Fueros (or provincial privileges) of those districts, and making their laws and customs conform to those of Castile. This measure had its grave disadvantages, because Valencia and Aragon still enjoyed a remnant of their ancient liberties, whilst Castile had long since been deprived of hers. Madame des Ursins, however, gave the measure her approval and powerful support. This is not surprising, since it was impossible for her to have any experience of constitutional government. She had, moreover, seen Spain torn by adverse factions and invaded by foreigners, and she would naturally suppose that a measure which promoted unity of action and undivided authority must be beneficial. The increase of power it must give to the King would also seem to her a great advantage. She had continually witnessed the evils produced by a too powerful aristocracy and an overbearing priesthood. She had seen prominent members of both these classes abandon the cause of Philip at its utmost need, and join the ranks of his enemies; and she was well aware that the King owed his triumphant return to his capital, not to the lords of Castile, but to the common people. Madame des Ursins saw these people frequently oppressed by the nobles and unable to obtain justice, and knew them to be overburdened by taxation, whilst the priests and nobles claimed their right of exemption and refused to contribute their share to the expenses of the State. To Madame des Ursins the best mode of remedying such evils seemed to consist in rendering the Sovereign independent alike of the nobility and of the provincial councils.

Amelot, in one of his despatches to Louis XIV. written at this period, remarks: "The time has now gone by when Philip V. had neither troops nor arms, nor yet artillery; when his very servants' wages were not paid; and when his half-starved bodyguard were thankful to obtain a share of the soup which was doled out to beggars at the convent doors. This state of things existed only four years ago." Affairs had indeed changed since then. The State credit was restored, a great and important victory won, and both invaders and rebels driven to the remoter parts of the kingdom. "Such was the result," declares François Combes, "of a succession of political and financial measures initiated by Madame des Ursins or carried into effect under her guidance."

CHAPTER X

JOY IN THE PALACE

THE victory of Almanza and its results released the Court of Madrid from all cause for immediate anxiety. Madame des Ursins' letters reflect this happier state of affairs. We find her occupied at this time with preparations for the arrival of the much-desired heir to the throne. She arranges for no fewer than twelve wet-nurses to be brought to Madrid in readiness for the important event. These were peasant women from the province of Biscay. Madame des Ursins thus describes their arrival at the palace of Buen Retiro, where she and the Queen were staying. "On their way here the nurses passed through the city of Madrid, where the people hailed them with delight and showered blessings on their heads. . . . I received them at the end of a gallery in the Queen's apartments. I saluted each one heartily, and then conducted them to her Majesty, who graciously stepped forward to meet them. At this moment all the babies, who were carried in their mothers' arms, set up a lusty roar! The women fell on their knees to kiss the Queen's hand; some were struck dumb with astonishment at their surroundings, others expressed their delight in a thousand simple and natural words, straight from the heart, which would have touched you as they did me. . . . Supper was then served for the nurses, and as I wished to make them feel at ease in my presence, I sat down myself at the head of the table, occupying a pretty wicker chair whilst the guests sat on the carpet after the manner of their country. I tasted the various dishes in order to ascertain that they were not too rich nor too highly flavoured, and finding them to my liking I took occasion to take my own supper with the nurses. We drank to the health of all the royal family and to the welfare of the prince about to be born.

Never did I partake of a more agreeable meal!"

The social creed of those days placed such an impassable gulf between a noble lady and a peasant woman that the above details amazed Madame de Maintenon, and she responds: "I do not believe that devotion to our royal family ever moved any one to carry kindness and condescension to such a point as you did, dear madame, in your reception of the nurses for the Prince of Asturias (for I earnestly hope the child will be a boy). I wish I could have been present at the feast. Nothing could have afforded me more pleasure. You are admirable in everything that you do, and are very sure to find an admirer in me."

In some of the letters of this period the two friends discuss matters relating to the management of infancy. Madame des Ursins expresses her disapproval of the plan of swathing infants upon a mattress. Referring to the absence of this practice among the English, she remarks, "The method followed in England must certainly be good, for nowhere do we find better shaped people than the English."

On August 25 the Queen of Spain gave birth to a son. Madame des Ursins writes the same day to Madame de Maintenon, dating her letter " Madrid, St. Louis's Day, 1707. My prophecies are now fulfilled. We have the finest prince in the world, and the Queen is doing excellently. The people have one and all remarked that God has favoured us with this gift on the Feast of St. Louis. . . . I embrace you, Madame, a thousand times, and wish you as much happiness for years to come as I possess this day." The *Gazette de France* of August 30 announces the birth of the Prince of Asturias, observing that the child "is handsome, well formed, and robust. . . . His Majesty (the King of Spain)," continues the Gazette, "has been pleased to grant liberty to all prisoners, excepting thieves, gipsies, and those who have merited death."

Madame de Maintenon responds to her friend's communication with cordial congratulations, and describes the joy experienced at

Versailles on the arrival of the good news. She dwells especially on the joy of the Duchess of Burgundy, the young Queen's sister. The Duchess had recently given birth to the infant Duke of Brittany, heir to the throne of France. Madame de Maintenon was as much interested in all that concerned this child as the Princess des Ursins was in the little Prince of Asturias. It is pleasant to come upon anecdotes of baby life in the midst of the subjects for grave reflection that fill so much of the correspondence of the two friends.

"Never has a child given fairer promise of life than our prince," writes Madame des Ursins. "Her Majesty already amuses herself with him as if she found him good company, and it is the prettiest sight in the world to see him in the arms of such a tender, gracious mother. From all that you do me the honour to relate, Madame, of the Duke of Brittany," she playfully continues, "I see plainly that the two cousins have each their partisan, and I begin to doubt if we shall manage to agree about them!" Often in the midst of accounts of battles or sieges, or of plans for raising funds for the army, Madame des Ursins will pause to make such remarks as the following: "Our little prince has just cut another tooth and we expect him soon to cut two or three more." "He already shows signs of an excellent disposition. If he gives me a little slap in play and I pretend to be hurt, he turns to kiss me with a sweetness of manner winning beyond expression, and with tears in his eyes which show the sorrow he feels for having given pain. If such a disposition be well developed he will be adored by his people." Speaking of children generally in one of her letters, she remarks: " I could pass my time very happily with them if I had not other matters to demand my attention. They have an innocence and gaiety of heart which charm me greatly, and which one hardly meets with elsewhere."

The tastes of Madame des Ursins and Madame de Maintenon differed greatly in one respect. Madame de Maintenon sought relief from the trials of her life in solitude and meditation, Madame des Ursins in intercourse with the enlightened men of her day. Madame de Maintenon so much disliked making new acquaintances, that her doors were usually closed to strangers, however distinguished they might be. Her friend remonstrates with her on the subject again and again. Alluding to her refusal to admit the Prince de Vaudemont, late Governor of Milan, to her "impenetrable apartments," Madame des Ursins writes: "Would it have been a misfortune, think you, to become well acquainted with such a man by conversing with him upon various subjects and hearing his thoughts and opinions? For my part, there is nothing I enjoy more keenly than drawing out the thoughts and opinions of those who have played a distinguished part in the world, and who, from their long experience, have had occasion to mark the prevailing characteristics of humanity. By this means we acquire knowledge that may be of great service. I know your predilection for solitude; but would to Heaven I could pursuade you to exclude yourself less from commerce with the world!"

Madame de Maintenon in her reply allows that perhaps she might have done well to see the Prince de Vaudemont, but adds, "You know, madame, how little I enjoy receiving visitors. You are the only person who ever caused me to change my sentiments on that point. I can never forget the pleasure I experienced in your society, and the eagerness with which I hastened to your quiet boudoir, which I should infinitely prefer at this moment were you in it, to all the fine grounds of Marly or Trianon!"

The two friends each suffered, at times, from ill health. Madame des Ursins invariably makes light of her ailments, though sometimes she must have been greatly inconvenienced by them. She was subject to a weakness in one of her eyes which often prevented her from writing. Most of her letters are dictated to her private secretary and friend d'Aubigny. When recovering from an attack of fever she writes to Madame de Maintenon: "If it was the will of fate that one of us should have the fever, it was well that I should be that one, for illness does not make me melancholy, and I have observed that you are always more cheerful when you are in good health." In another letter she remarks, "There is a right time for most things, but surely none for melancholy."

Madame de Maintenon suffered much from rheumatism, which was aggravated by the cold draughts of air that circulated through the great palaces in which she lived. This over-ventilation was encouraged by Louis XIV.'s love of fresh air. On one occasion Madame des Ursins sends a folding-screen to her friend and begs her to make use of it as a protection against the cutting draughts at Fontainebleau; but the gift was declined. Even Madame de Maintenon's power at Court was insufficient to introduce such a simple innovation. The old King held rigid views as to the disposition of the furniture in his apartments, where all was arranged in formal order, and where no change was permitted. "Do not suppose for a moment, dear madame," writes Madame de Maintenon, "that I can have screens placed between me and the great windows of my apartments. It is not possible to arrange a room according to one's own liking which the King enters every day. *Il faut périr en symétrie.*"

On one occasion, Madame de Maintenon having mentioned that she was going to be bled, Madame des Ursins responds, "If you mean to be bled pray conceal the fact from me. I am fully persuaded, in spite of all that Monsieur Fagon * may say to the contrary, that nothing tends so much to shorten life as the practice of bleeding, and I desire the preservation of your life as much as I do that of my own."

In one of her letters Madame des Ursins expresses regret that her friend should be debarred by illness from enjoying the grounds of Fontainebleau. She wishes she herself could be there, "for," she observes, "I always enjoy long rambles, especially in forest glades, whose solitude has a great charm for me." Alluding to the gardens of the Trianon, she writes: "I often walked over to them from Versailles,

* The Court physician.

sometimes early in the morning, sometimes in the afternoon, and enjoyed the sweet perfume of the flowers. I greatly admired both the palace and the grounds. Indeed, the place seemed to me to be enchanted. . . . I remember your once telling me, dear Madame," she observes, "that you cared little for stately mansions and fine grounds. Our tastes differ in that respect, for I take a keen pleasure in them." In another letter Madame des Ursins refers to Louis XIV. having given up the erection of some buildings which he had planned, on account of the expense entailed; she goes on to say: "I can understand the sacrifice better than most people, for there is no occupation I relish more than that of altering and embellishing mansions. I have effected such trifling changes as lay in my power in this palace. They have cost little, but have added much to the comfort of the King and Queen. The occupation has enabled me to pass many an hour pleasantly that might otherwise have seemed tedious." Madame des Ursins, we are told, greatly improved the grounds of the palace of Buen Retiro by introducing plantations of fine trees.

Many and various are the subjects touched upon by the two friends in their correspondence. Alluding to the strife between the Jansenists and the Jesuits, Madame des Ursins writes: "They would do well, I think, to lay aside their bickerings until such time as peace is restored to our countries. After that they might recommence their private warfare and tear each others' eyes out anew, but for the present there are more serious affairs to occupy public attention. For my own part, I regard both parties with so little favour that I have no desire to hear of their doings, and I make a point of choosing my confessor from among those ecclesiastics who neither love nor hate either party."

CHAPTER XI

REVERSES

A RUMOUR was afloat at this time that Madame des Ursins and the Duke of Berwick were at variance. There seems to have been no foundation for it. "The Duke of Berwick," writes Madame des Ursins, "writes to me in a more obliging and friendly way than ever, and yet it is reported in Paris that we have quarrelled with each other. One needs to be well armed with patience to endure all these ridiculous calumnies. . . . There are people who delight in evil speaking, and their statements are often more readily credited than the statements of their honest neighbours. . . . Happy those who can pass their lives in peace and retirement!"

Madame de Maintenon responds, "We learn

from all quarters, dear madame, that nothing can be more untrue than the reports respecting the Duke of Berwick and yourself. . . . One must make up one's mind to live with people who are malicious, ungrateful, and treacherous, since the world is full of them, and since they abound especially in Courts, where contending interests naturally give rise to evil passions."

A few months later, when it was believed that the Duke of Berwick was likely to be removed from his command in Spain, Madame des Ursins wrote to Mons. de Torcy (Minister for Foreign Affairs at Versailles) : "If we are to credit public rumour we are about to lose Marshal Berwick. It is affirmed that he is to return to France to assume command of the troops in Dauphiné. The King and Queen are at a loss, sir, to imagine why a General should be taken away from them whose services they had especially desired, and whose presence is necessary to their well-being, owing to his thorough knowledge of all matters connected with the war in this country; a general, too, who is universally loved by the Spaniards. . . .

We endeavour to disbelieve the report, but should it prove true, the results will be most pernicious." Unfortunately it did prove true, and Berwick was withdrawn in the autumn of 1707.

But still greater evils were in store for Spain. Louis XIV. had for some time past been making secret overtures to the Allies. The result of his negotiations was a treaty for the neutrality of Italy, known as the Treaty of Milan. The French garrisons were, in consequence, withdrawn from the Milanese towns, and the Austrian troops were set at liberty to march southwards for the conquest of Naples. This they soon accomplished.

The Princess des Ursins writes to Madame de Maintenon: "I cannot think of the sad fatality by which the State of Milan was lost, and which led to all the other losses in Italy, without heartfelt sorrow. I feel profound pity for the good subjects of our Catholic King. Some of the Neapolitan nobles have evinced their zeal and fidelity in such a striking and touching manner that they merit the highest reward. The Duke of Popoli, captain of the guards, is one of these. He is devoted to his royal master, and he esteems as nothing all the sacrifices he has made for the sake of his duty."

In the summer of 1708 the island of Sardinia was lost to the Spanish crown. It was captured by the English with little difficulty, as the inhabitants were already disaffected towards Philip V. The only attempt at opposition was made by a native gentleman, Don Vicente Bacallar, but his efforts were fruitless. This gentleman was afterwards created Marquis de San Phélipe by Philip V., and under that title he is known as the best contemporary historian of the War of the Spanish Succession in Spain.

The loss of Sardinia was followed by that of the island of Minorca, whose chief harbour, Port Mahon, was a place of great importance. "The loss of Port Mahon," observes Madame des Ursins, " is most serious. The enemy will now harass our trade in the Mediterranean, and will threaten our very coasts."

France was suffering no less than Spain at this period. A large army had been raised with incredible difficulty, and sent into Flanders under the command of Vendôme and the Duke of Burgundy. But these two leaders, who were diametrically opposed in character and principles, could not work in unison, and they were defeated at every encounter with Marlborough and Prince Eugene. At last the important frontier town of Lille was captured by the enemy, and the very capital of France threatened. To add to the general distress, the winter of 1708-9 set in with unusual severity. The cold, St. Simon tells us, was greater than had ever before been experienced. "In four days [after the commencement of the frost]," he writes, "the Seine and all the other rivers were frozen over, and for the first time the sea was turned to ice all along our coasts." This severe cold lasted for nearly three months. The fruit-trees throughout France were killed, and the grain perished beneath the soil. Money was scarce and famine seemed imminent. A letter from Madame de Maintenon to the Duc de Noailles reflects the general gloom. She writes: "Affliction and bitterness of spirit prevail on all sides—in the Church and in the State; in great matters and in small; among men and among women, in business and in private life, in society at large and in the family circle—all is affliction and bitterness of spirit."*

"The fall of Lille," writes Madame des Ursins, "has astonished this Court. . . . My heart bleeds at the news, and I confess that I can scarcely recognise my own nation, so changed it seems from what it once was. A noble desire for glory once inspired our people, but now they seem insensible to such a motive."

Louis XIV. wrote to Philip declaring that "the loss of Lille must put an end to all thoughts of peace, and that both he and his grandson must make renewed efforts to secure to Philip his possession of the crown of Spain. Madame des Ursins, who had begun to suspect double-dealing on the part of Louis, now writes to Madame de Maintenon: "His Catholic Majesty would not willingly suspect that these words are insincere and that the King is de-

* "Mémoires de Noailles."

luding him with false hopes, whilst in reality he intends entering into such another treaty with the enemy as that of Milan : of that treaty, as you are well aware, Madame, the King of Spain had no knowledge whatever."

Madame des Ursins further perceived that Louis XIV. was becoming weary of upholding his grandson's cause, and she endeavoured by every argument in her power to prevent his abandoning it. The Duke of Orleans, who had been sent to Spain as Generalissimo of the Forces in the place of the Duke of Berwick, was now in Paris on an embassy to the King. The Princess des Ursins writes to Madame de Maintenon : " The Duke of Orleans will represent to the King the terrible evils which must accrue to France as well as to Spain if the cause of his Catholic Majesty is abandoned. The arguments [which prove this] are so powerful and so well supported by facts, that I cannot doubt their making an impression upon the mind and heart of the King. I hope earnestly that his Majesty's long and glorious career may not now be tarnished by his subscribing to an ignoble peace. Surely the counsels of those who advocate such a measure should be repudiated with indignation!"

Madame de Maintenon herself, however, was beginning to desire peace at any price. "Our enemies triumph on all sides," she writes, "but we must bow our heads and submit to the strokes of the Almighty. . . . We are at Marly. In this delicious spot we hear now of nothing but sorrow and suffering. No poor countryman can be as absorbed as we are in questions concerning the condition of the crops and the price of corn which mounts higher and higher. Few market days pass without riots. . . . I used to think," she adds, "that no evil could be greater than the war, but the approaching famine is infinitely worse. Could you witness our condition you would blame us less and pity us more."

"You are indeed to be pitied," responds her friend, "and I can assure you that your sufferings afflict me as much as they do yourself. But beyond this I have to witness the sufferings of a King and Queen whose virtues I know and realize more fully than you can do, and whom I certainly love better than it is possible for any one else to love. If I appear unwilling to believe all that you desire me to believe it is not that I doubt your power of discernment nor your good intentions, but that I desire by my arguments, whether good or bad, to arouse the courage of those about you who are now giving way to depression."

"Your courage and resolution are marvellous!" exclaims Madame de Maintenon in reply, "but to what do they tend? Is your enterprise practicable? . . . You hold, dear madame, that we should perish rather than surrender. I hold that we should yield to the superior force of our enemies, and above all to the mighty arm of God, which is now visibly turned against us."

"Is it possible," writes Madame des Ursins (April 1, 1709), "that all your able men are at their wit's end?—that not one of them can devise a helpful measure? It is a proof of faint-hearted dejection that does them little credit, for great minds rise above difficulties and manfully resist the attacks of evil fortune. God can work miracles at all times, and the miracle I pray for now is that a spirit of courage and hopefulness may be revived in your Court, and that unity and concord may be restored to those personages in power who are now at variance."

The Princess des Ursins was certainly herself one of those whose powers of mind and character were manifested in times of trial. She now carefully thought out and suggested such plans as seemed likely to afford relief to the general distress. She forwarded a memorial to the Court of Versailles containing a scheme for raising money on good security, drawn up probably under her supervision, and which had been seen and approved by Amelot. In her letters on this subject she displays an accurate knowledge of the state of the finances of both France and Spain, and also of the condition of the crops in these countries. Madame des Ursins sent the memorial through Marshal Villeroy, who showed it to the Ministers and also to Madame de Maintenon. The latter was alarmed at the novel measures it advocated, and wrote to her friend: "Is it possible, think you, for a King to change in a moment the forms of government that he has maintained for sixty years? And how can we militate against the dearth of money and of food which are God's scourges? . . . The state to which France is reduced would fill you with grief could you behold it." The Princess des Ursins responds by vindicating the sound policy of the financial scheme, and then remarks: "Do not imagine, dear Madame, that I underrate the evils to which France is exposed. Our opinions on that head differ only in so far as I am persuaded that there are remedies at hand, and that if we perish it is by our own fault." The French Ministers shared Madame de Maintenon's dread of innovation in financial measures, and they therefore rejected the scheme at first sight. "They had at least the satisfaction," observes Ste. Beuve, "of perishing in the old grooves, since they would not leave them for new."

Madame des Ursins endeavoured to lessen

the strength of the enemy by suggesting a scheme which might induce the Duke of Savoy to quit the side of the Allies and join that of the Bourbons. He was greatly harassed at that time by the Austrian invasion of Italy, which threatened his own frontiers, so there seemed to be a chance of success.

Madame des Ursins' alert mind was ready to take advantage of every opportunity that might arise to improve the state of affairs. "She kept a keen eye," writes François Combes, "upon all that passed—upon foreign politics, upon the war, upon the movements and the sustenance of the troops, upon questions of finance, and upon the augmentation of the royal power, just as if she had been Regent of Spain."

It has been already remarked that the French troops were so ill paid as to be dependent on the Spanish Government for the necessaries of life. In spite of this fact, however, the Duke of Orleans was loud in his complaints against the Spaniards for the meagreness with which his troops were supplied and his anger was especially directed against the Princess des Ursins. On one memorable occasion, recorded by St. Simon, the Duke gave public expression to his anger. It was at a great banquet in Madrid, when he proposed a mock toast, using coarse epithets intended to designate the Princess des Ursins and her friend Madame de Maintenon. His meaning was too obvious to be mistaken and his wit too keen not to excite laughter. From that day forward all social intercourse between the Camarera-Mayor and the Duke was at an end.

In her endeavours to prevent Louis XIV. from abandoning the cause of Philip V., Madame des Ursins was earnestly seconded by Amelot, who pointed out to his Sovereign that the mere rumour of his desertion was already doing great harm. But the old King was bowed down by the trials that beset France, and he declared that "peace must be obtained at any price." The Allies demanded, as a first condition, that Philip should be withdrawn from Spain, and the Archduke Charles proclaimed King in his stead. "It is impossible," writes Louis to his Ambassador, "for the war to cease as long as he (Philip) remains on the throne of Spain. This is a painful declaration for you to convey to the King, but it is the truth, and, painful as it is, must be made known to him." Louis goes on to advise that his grandson should renounce the kingdoms of Spain and of the Indies, and content himself henceforth with reigning over the remnant of the Spanish dominions in Italy.

CHAPTER XII

LEFT TO FIGHT ALONE

Louis XIV.'s message came as a thunderbolt upon the palace of Madrid. For a moment Philip's courage wavered, and he was almost ready to accept the hard terms demanded by the Allies. But he had a counsellor at hand over whom fear had no dominion. The Princess des Ursins, we are told, addressed him in these words: "How is this, sire? Are you a king? Are you a man?—you, who value so lightly your sovereignty and who evince more weakness than a woman!"* Such words had their desired effect: Philip's courage was rekindled, and he wrote a letter to his grandfather declaring that he would rather die than renounce the throne of Spain and abandon his subjects.

* Histoire secrète de la cour de Madrid, année 1709.

The excitement in the city of Madrid was great when it became known that Louis XIV. was actually in treaty with the enemy with a view to handing over Spain and the Indies to the Archduke. "The effect which the tidings produced upon the grandees," writes the author of the "Mémoires de Noailles," "was strange and unexpected, and brought into light the hidden energy that underlies the Spanish character. The grandees not only denounced the conduct of Louis XIV., declaring that he was robbing them of a King whom he had himself placed upon their throne, but they professed themselves ready to sacrifice both their lives and their property in support of the cause of Philip V." The Duc d'Arcos, as well as many of the other grandees who now stepped forward to the rescue, had been far from satisfied with the Government, the interference of France being a constant source of irritation to their pride. Now, for the first time, they were in a position to defend their King against the manœuvres of France, and this circumstance united them in one body for determined action.

Madame des Ursins fully comprehended the critical state of affairs. She saw that the time was come when Spain must act independently of France, and she counselled Philip to throw himself unreservedly into the arms of the Spanish nation and to trust to the professions of attachment now made by the grandees regardless of what their former sentiments might have been. In pursuance of this advice Philip called a meeting of his Ministers and nobles, and "declared to them his firm resolution not to renounce the throne of Spain," assuring them that he "counted upon their fidelity as he did upon that of the people at large, and that he felt sure they would not abandon him." Philip's auditors responded cordially to this appeal. They declared "that if the King of France was compelled to withdraw his troops they would strain every nerve to supply their loss, that they would never suffer England and Holland to dispose of the Spanish crown, and that the whole nation, rich and poor alike, would take up arms and fight to the death in defence of their King, their country, and their honour." *

During this crisis of affairs great agitation prevailed among all classes. Louis XIV.'s conduct had suddenly reawakened the old feeling of hostility towards the French nation. Outrages were daily expected, and it became necessary that some measure should be passed that would reassure the Spaniards and calm public feeling. The Princess des Ursins took the initiative. She caused a royal decree to be issued banishing all Frenchmen from Spain. This was indeed throwing Philip into the arms of his subjects and making a direct appeal to the ancient loyalty of the Spanish nation. "The event," writes Geffroy, "justified this generous policy." The effect it produced at Versailles can be readily imagined. The anger of the Court was directed against the Camarera-Mayor, and rumours were soon afloat of a second recall. But she continued her course with courage and firmness.

A change of Ministry in Spain had become

* "Mémoires de Noailles."

necessary on account of the altered condition of affairs. Madame des Ursins turned to the national party, and chose the Duc de Medina-Cœli as the leader of the new Ministry. The Duke had been formerly a member of Charles II.'s Cabinet and was one of the most powerful noblemen in Spain. But he was proud, suspicious, and easily offended, and had of late kept aloof from public affairs. Still, Madame des Ursins had always contrived to be on good terms with him, and she felt convinced that the special circumstances of the time made it necessary that he should be selected as a prominent upholder of Philip V. The Duke was therefore given the post of Minister for Foreign Affairs.

An assembly of the representatives of the State was now called to take the oath of allegiance to the infant heir to the throne. The ceremony took place on April 7, 1709, amid great rejoicings. This function, besides strengthening feelings of loyalty to the Bourbon dynasty, was an act of defiance to those who imagined that its reign was coming to an end.

In the following June Louis XIV. issued an order for the withdrawal of all his troops from Spain. We find Madame des Ursins writing at once to Chamillart to obtain some mitigation of the decree, and at her instance some battalions were left behind under the command of Marshal Besons. Louis was the more willing to make this concession as the Spanish Government offered to pay his troops. He also saw the danger of suddenly leaving the Spanish frontier of France unprotected.

The old King was sorely pressed at this time by troubles both within and without his kingdom. The terms of peace demanded by the Allies "were needlessly harsh," as our own historians admit. Louis was required "not only to withdraw all help from Philip V., but actually to assist in driving him out of Spain." Large concessions were also demanded in the Netherlands — notably the surrender of five cities belonging to the Spanish crown. Louis urged Philip, through his Ambassador, to give up these cities, and told him that "if he refused to do so, he (Louis) feared he might be obliged to agree to one of the conditions [of peace] most repulsive to him, namely, to join his forces with those of the enemy and take the cities by storm."* But in spite of this declaration the mind of Louis recoiled from such a course. He made an appeal to his subjects to enable him to continue the war and to reject the humiliating terms of the Allies. The appeal was not made in vain; "the cry for peace was hushed," and the negotiations with the enemy were broken off in June 1709. But France was not in a position to help Spain, and from this time forward the two countries began to act more independently of each other.

The French Ambassador Amelot sent in his resignation to the Court of Versailles. Madame des Ursins writes to the Maréchale de Noailles: "I am about to lose Monsieur Amelot. I am sorry for this, not only on account of the loss it occasions to the service of the King and Queen, but because our intercourse has always been that of friends who have perfect confidence in each other."

* "Mémoires de Noailles."

A new danger now arose from a quarter little suspected by the general public—namely, from the Duke of Orleans, who had recently held the high post of Generalissimo of the Spanish and French Forces. The Duke had secretly formed the design of getting possession of the throne of Spain for himself. He was, like Philip V., distantly related to Charles II. of Spain; but Philip had the prior claim to the succession as belonging to the elder branch of the Bourbon family. The Duke actually entered into secret negotiations with the Allies, offering to make various concessions to them if they would make him King of Spain instead of their protégé the Archduke Charles. The negotiations were carried on with General Stanhope, who in former times had been on friendly terms with the Duke. "Stanhope received," writes Lord Mahon, " a confidential overture, and afterwards several secret visits from Monsieur Flotte, one of the Duke's aides-de-camp." This Flotte and a man named Rénaut were employed to carry on the intrigue, as the Duke of Orleans himself was not at that time in Spain.

General Stanhope reported the Duke's proposals to the English Government, and suggested that it would be well to make use of this plot to detach the Duke of Orleans from the side of their enemies. The negotiations therefore continued. But the English were only making a tool of the Duke, as the Spanish historian San Phélipe has pointed out. "It was not to their interest," he remarks, "to have a prince of the House of Bourbon on the throne of Spain, and whether that prince called himself Philip or Louis was merely the question of a name."

The affair was carried on with the utmost secrecy, but a vigilant eye was upon the Duke of Orleans. The Princess des Ursins knew his character and mistrusted him. "She read the very secrets of his heart," writes San Phélipe, "and was the first to suspect that, although quitting Spain himself, the Duke had left agents behind him to carry on his designs." She discovered that Flotte paid visits during the night to the camp of General Stanhope, and she discovered also that Rénaut was intriguing amongst the disaffected in Madrid. "The

DUKE OF ORLEANS (AFTERWARDS REGENT OF FRANCE)

Princess des Ursins watched every secret movement," observes Lord Mahon, "she caught every unguarded word; and above all, gave herself full time to complete and mature her proofs, well knowing that in political affairs it is almost incredible how much time may be lost by hurry and precipitation. At length, having awaited the favourable opportunity and obtained the authorisation of Philip, she gave orders for arresting first Rénaut at Madrid, and afterwards Flotte at the Spanish camp in Aragon. Their papers were seized and found to contain several writings in an unknown cipher, and parts of the correspondence between the Duke of Orleans and Stanhope."

When the affair became public it aroused a widespread feeling of indignation against the Duke. Philip gave vent to his feelings in a letter to Louis XIV., to which Louis replied by endeavouring to excuse as far as possible the conduct of his nephew. St. Simon observes: "I have never been able fully to unravel the threads of this intrigue, and still less have I been able to discover how much of it was previously known to the King." That Louis found himself in a difficult position is certain. Had the Duke been less nearly related to himself, severe measures would probably have been taken, but as it was, the affair was gradually hushed up. Louis informed his grandson that "he had been obliged, under the circumstances, to show a clemency which, he admitted, was not quite consistent with justice."* He, however, showed personal displeasure to his nephew, who remained under a cloud for long afterwards. So ended the Duke's schemes for sovereignty in Spain.

* François Combes.

CHAPTER XIII

TREACHERY IN THE CAMP

THE Duke of Orleans' plot against Philip V. failed, as we have seen, but its evil effects still lingered. Marshal Besons, who acted as commander-in-chief of the Spanish and French troops in the north-eastern part of Spain, was a friend and protégé of the Duke's, and he secretly resented the arrest of his patron's agents. His army was well appointed, and his soldiers were eager to fight the Austrians, who were quartered near to them on the open plains beyond Lerida. But Besons refused to avail himself of the most favourable opportunities to do battle, and, though greatly superior to the enemy in numbers, resolutely remained inactive. At last Besons actually suffered the enemy to cross the river Ségres before his very eyes, capture Fort Belaguay, and take three of his battalions prisoners,

The news of this affair aroused a burst of indignation at Madrid. Madame des Ursins gave vent to her feelings in the two following letters, where, under terms of apparent respect towards Louis XIV., her real opinion of his equivocal conduct is very evident. "Marshal Besons," she writes to Madame de Maintenon (September 1, 1709), "may have acted in obedience to the King [of France] . . . but we cannot attribute the responsibility to his Majesty without failing in the respect which we owe to him. It is impossible to believe that a being possessing a character so lofty could be capable of tarnishing his reputation by a deed which must be detested by all honest men. For these reasons, Madame, their Catholic Majesties throw all the blame upon the General, being unable to imagine that the King, his master, could have ordered him to commit such an act of cowardice. If the King chooses to abandon his grandson, cost what it may to France and to her people who are dishonouring themselves, there is nothing more to be said; but if at any rate the King does not himself wish to promote his grandson's downfall, surely as long as his troops are left in Spain, in the pay of his Catholic Majesty, they should prevent the enemy from passing over our rivers when we are far stronger in every respect than they are. . . . The King [of Spain] leaves Madrid to-morrow, determined to die rather than to allow himself to be covered with infamy."

The second letter is addressed to the Maréchale de Noailles, and was despatched the following day. "The King of Spain," writes Madame des Ursins, "has started this morning in all haste for Aragon, in order to place himself at the head of his army. He is full of indignation at the conduct of Marshal Besons, which is equally injurious to the Spanish cause and disgraceful to the French. It appears that the Marshal was not even content with refusing to fight the enemy when they offered him the best opportunity in the world for so doing, and were greatly inferior in numbers, but that he actually fled before them, . . . abandoning both the troops and forts that belong to his Majesty. The Spanish people are so much incensed at the whole affair that it is impossible to say what they may do. They declare aloud that their King has been betrayed, and that there is a plot on foot to snatch his crown from his head. Appearances certainly justify their assertions, and do little honour to our [French] nation."

Madame de Maintenon, in her reply to her friend's letter, calls it a "letter of blood and fire." She laments the cause that has provoked it, but evidently fears to censure Besons' conduct. Nor was it censured by Louis XIV. The same reasons which had led the King to condone the offence of the Duke of Orleans led him to condone that of his protégé. But Besons had made himself too unpopular to remain in Spain, and before long he was replaced by another commander.

The intercourse of Madame des Ursins and Madame de Maintenon was somewhat embittered at this period by their widely different views. Madame de Maintenon persisted in believing that all efforts to retain the throne of Spain for Philip V. were vain, and that the hand of God was visibly turned against the Bourbons. "It is resisting His will," she writes, "to offer opposition to peace. I fully appreciate your attachment to their Catholic Majesties, but do you wish to ruin France and to see the English in Paris? . . . Peace alone can save us. The famine grows worse every day. We have no supplies and shall all starve in the winter if the sea is not thrown open to us as a passage for corn. How little could I have foretold," she adds, "even when most beset with fears, that we should be reduced so low as actually to wish to see the King and Queen of Spain dethroned!"

Madame des Ursins, could answer even this letter with her usual courage and cheerfulness. Alluding to the gallant conduct of the French in a recent defeat in Flanders, she writes: "The Allies will be obliged to change their ill-opinion of the French nation, and can no longer count on invading their country with impunity. . . . But I forget, dear Madame," she remarks playfully, "that these poor French have forfeited your esteem, and that you fear they will be unable to prevent the terrible enemy from penetrating to Versailles! If your courtiers would but cease to lament and to predict misfortunes, things might well take a turn for the better and money begin to circulate once more. I admit that the dearth of food is a grievous evil, but you must remember that long before it existed the courtiers made the same lamentations. They declared more than four years ago that all would be lost unless the whole Spanish kingdom and a great part of the King [of France's] own territory were thrown into the jaws of our enemies, and that if this were done we might hope they would be kind enough to forbear devouring the remainder of France! . . . Your faith," she concludes, "is too narrow. Mine has a far wider scope, for I am persuaded that Heaven will continue to be gracious to us . . . provided we endeavour to merit its favours by neglecting nothing that depends on our own exertions."

But Madame de Maintenon could not brave

the trials of the terrible year 1709, and she began to be weary of Madame des Ursins' persistent championship of Philip V. and her reiterated arguments against the acceptance of the terms of peace offered by the Allies. In one of her letters Madame des Ursins, after treating this subject at some length, had proceeded to vindicate the principles of the financial scheme recently forwarded by her to the Court of Versailles and there rejected. Madame de Maintenon replies with an affectation of humility which she sometimes assumed, "Your letter is so far above my powers of intellect that I am sorry it should have been addressed to me. . . . I cannot venture to show it [to those in authority]. People here do not approve of women giving their opinion upon public affairs." This observation, coming as it did from a woman whose invisible hand had held the reins of power in France for nearly thirty years, nettled Madame des Ursins, and she ironically retorted: "If women's expressing their opinion upon public affairs is disapproved of in France, so much the better. If we are to be allowed no share in State matters we shall at least be able to hold men responsible for all that goes wrong. It seems to me," she adds, "that ways of thinking must have greatly changed at Versailles since I was there, for the King appeared to me to hold widely different sentiments when I had the honour of conversing with him."

We have seen how, through the Princess des Ursins' influence, the Duc de Medina-Cœli had been given the most important post in the Ministry. She was not blind to his character. She knew that he had, like many of the grandees, caballed against Philip's rule, and even suspected him of approving the Duke of Orleans' plot. His elevation was a bold measure, but the critical state of affairs justified boldness. In April 1710, not many months afterwards, the Duc de Medina-Cœli was suddenly arrested and thrown into prison. He was accused of high treason. The principal evidence against him is given by the historian San Phélipe. An expedition for the recovery of the island of Sardinia had been planned by the

Spanish Government in which San Phélipe was to take part. In the meantime he was engaged in assisting in the preparations which were being made at Genoa. The Duc de Medina-Cœli entrusted the command of the expedition to the Duc d'Uzeda, a man already suspected of favouring the Austrian cause. San Phélipe declares that the Duc d'Uzeda had several secret interviews with the Austrian Envoy at Genoa and also with the English Ambassador, and that he betrayed to them the secret of the projected expedition, and thus caused its total failure. When Medina-Cœli was arrested, a correspondence in cypher between him and D'Uzeda was discovered among his private papers. But the whole affair was involved in a good deal of mystery, which, we are told, has never been quite cleared up. It is certain, however, that the party of the Duke of Orleans in Madrid looked upon Medina-Cœli as one of their supporters, for they resented his fall as a blow to their patron's cause. Their anger was directed chiefly against Madame des Ursins, and they succeeded in raising a new cabal against her in the Court of Versailles, where her opposition to peace made her unpopular. Her recall was pressed for, and at one time seemed to be imminent.

Madame des Ursins' conduct during this crisis of her affairs was dignified as usual. She considered her plans for the future in case of her retirement from public life, and held herself in readiness for whatever turn fortune might take. "I am by no means dependent for happiness," she writes to Marshal Villeroy, "upon the titles and grandeur which fortune bestows. I could pass without any difficulty, I assure you, from the act of guiding a State to that of guiding a plough." But before long affairs took a new turn in her favour, and her position at Madrid was once again rendered secure.

Meanwhile Philip V. had joined the campaign in Aragon, where for the first time during these long wars he and his rival, the Archduke Charles, met face to face. A battle was fought at Saragossa on August 20, 1710, in which Philip's army sustained a severe defeat.

About four thousand men were left dead on the battle-field, and as many more taken prisoners. Philip himself escaped with difficulty. The Archduke entered Saragossa in triumph, and was acknowledged King throughout Aragon. Philip returned in all haste to Madrid to take measures for defending his capital, as the enemy was preparing to march southward.

When the news of the disaster reached Paris it aroused a fresh outcry against the war and a reiterated demand for peace at any price. Louis XIV. considered that the cause of the Bourbons in Spain was lost, and he determined to make a fresh effort to persuade his grandson to accept the terms of peace offered by the Allies. The Duc de Noailles, who was then in Spain, was commissioned confidentially to promote this end. There exists a letter from Torcy (Minister for Foreign Affairs) to the Duke, containing instructions to him to use every means in his power to induce Philip to renounce the sovereignty of Spain and of the Indies, and to accept in lieu of them the remnant of the Italian dominions belonging to the Spanish crown. "In order to attain your object," writes Torcy, "you must endeavour to win over the Princess des Ursins to your side. There is no doubt that she is disinterestedly attached to the King and Queen of Spain. Urge her to make use of her influence over them to second your views. After you have employed all the arguments suggested by the necessity of the case . . . do not scruple to employ any further means of persuasion that you may deem likely to succeed. . . . Possibly the Princess may not be insensible to her own personal interests. . . . I leave you free to offer her any recompense that you think she would most value to bring her to our purpose. If, however, the promise of rewards and the promise also of the King's [of France] assured protection cannot move her, do not hesitate to frighten her by the declaration that the King will look upon her henceforth as the cause of his grandson's ruin. Tell her (but this only in case of dire necessity) that his Majesty is well aware of the absolute control she possesses over the mind of the

Catholic King; and that the firmness evinced by him in his letters and conversations regarding the throne of Spain is her handiwork. It is on *her* shoulders, therefore, that his Majesty will lay the blame, if his grandson is hurried on to loss and failure while there still remains a course open to him by which a part of his possessions may yet be saved."

Madame des Ursins' response to such overtures was to inspire Philip V. with yet more courage to defend his throne against the attacks of both friends and foes. Philip wrote a spirited letter to his grandfather (penned possibly by herself), declaring that "no arguments of the Duc de Noailles could change his determination to die rather than to abandon Spain."

This decision was looked upon at Versailles as final, and no further attempt was made to induce Philip V. to reverse it, although the results of the defeat of Saragossa seemed to threaten the cause with total ruin.

CHAPTER XIV

A CAUSE WON

IN the beginning of September 1710 the army of the Allies had approached so near to Madrid as to necessitate a second flight of the royal family from their capital. Valladolid was chosen this time as the city of refuge, and thither the King and Queen and their infant son repaired, accompanied by Madame des Ursins, the Ministers of State, the Judges, and the Court. Philip's misfortunes, far from damping the ardour of his subjects, aroused a fresh spirit of loyalty and attachment in all classes. This was especially remarked in the nobility. The grandees, who as a body had stood aloof from him in 1706, now eagerly gathered round him. " Nearly thirty thousand persons are said to have crowded the road to

Valladolid. Even ladies of high rank were seen to follow on foot rather than not follow at all."* When the Archduke Charles made his triumphal entry into Madrid, he found a silent and abandoned town. Shops, manufactories, and private houses were all closed, and hardly an inhabitant to be seen. "This city is a desert!" exclaimed the Archduke, and, deeply mortified at such a reception, he ordered the procession to halt and to disperse. He now tried every means in his power to gain new adherents to his cause, sparing neither money nor promises of high honours, but in vain. "Nothing could shake the stubborn loyalty of the people, and very few men of rank and influence espoused his cause." The Marquis de Mancera, a statesman of the venerable age of one hundred years, had been obliged by his infirmities to remain behind his master at Madrid, but his spirit was undaunted. When General Stanhope endeavoured to persuade him to acknowledge the Archduke as King of Spain, he replied, " Sir, I have but one God

* Lord Mahon.

and but one King; and during my short remnant of life I am determined to be faithful to both." *

Ever since the withdrawal of the Duke of Berwick, Spain had sorely needed a wise and able commander-in-chief. The Spanish generals who succeeded him had not sufficient experience in warfare to fit them for the highest post of command. The Princess des Ursins, ever alive to the needs of Spain, had written to the Court of Versailles, even before the flight from Madrid took place, to urge that the Duc de Vendôme should be sent to Spain to take command of the army. He had held that post in 1702, and was popular with the Spanish nation. She wrote a letter to the Duke himself on September 8, in which she remarks: "I have so much confidence in your ability that, if his Majesty [the King of France] will consent to your coming, I make no doubt you will completely change the state of affairs in this country. In the meantime, sir, we are greatly in need of your wise counsels." A month

* Lord Mahon.

later the grandees themselves drew up a petition to Louis XIV., urging him to send the Duc de Vendôme to take command of the Spanish army. Louis at last gave his consent, and the Duke was sent to Spain, being provided at the same time with a large reinforcement of French troops. He reached Castile by the end of September, and after stopping at Valladolid to concert measures with the Court, proceeded with his battalions to join the Spanish army.

Vendôme's first care was to prevent a junction of the Imperialists with the Portuguese who were advancing from the frontiers of Portugal. This he succeeded in doing, and the result of his manœuvre was to render the Archduke's position at Madrid so insecure that he had to abandon the city. The Archduke and his followers had experienced great difficulty in remaining there even for a few weeks. "Straitened for want of supplies, debarred from all communication with Aragon or the sea," their conviction became daily stronger that "Castile, a country of open plains and resolute inhabitants, may soon be overrun but never subdued. They found it a morsel easy to swallow, but hard to digest." * As Charles retreated from Madrid on the morning of November 9, he had the mortification of witnessing the satisfaction of the inhabitants at his departure and of hearing it announced by the joyful ringing of the city bells.

On December 3 Philip re-entered his capital. "He was received with something better than pomp or pageant—the loud, repeated, and affectionate acclamations of his people. Eager to behold him, their throngs encumbered his carriage and delayed his progress; and the city, which all day resounded with their loyal greetings, at night blazed forth in a general illumination. On his part, Philip gave every token of his gratitude and attachment to his brave Castilians." † He paid a visit to the old Marquis di Mancera to thank him for his loyalty, and it is recorded by St. Simon (that chronicler of Court ceremonial) that this was the only visit paid by a King of Spain to a subject since the days of Philip II., when that

* Lord Mahon. † *Ibid.*

monarch visited the Duke of Alva on his deathbed. But Philip could not remain long at Madrid. He hastened to join his army at Guadalaxara.

On December 10 a great battle was fought at Villaviciosa, a town on the river Tajuna, not many miles north of Guadalaxara, and this time the cause of Philip V. was triumphant. Madame des Ursins writes to a friend from Vittoria, whither the Court had removed temporarily: " The King of Spain has just achieved a complete victory over Count Staremberg, after a battle fought with the utmost valour on both sides. We have taken three thousand prisoners, killed and wounded a vast number, and seized all the artillery and baggage wagons of the enemy. On the same day . . . eight battalions and eight squadrons of English soldiers, under the command of Generals Stanhope, Carpenter, and Wills, who had entrenched themselves in Brihuaga, were forced to lay down their arms. In short, nothing could be more glorious nor more full of promise for the future than this victory."

"The zeal and enthusiasm displayed by the grandees on this occasion," writes François Combes, "can hardly be described. Their desire to distinguish themselves and to atone for past indifference, rebellion, or treason was so great, that when some regiments of raw recruits fled in panic before the enemy, their officers (the flower of the Spanish nobility) pressed forward to take their places in the ranks, formed a compact line to protect the centre, and fought like lions." When night fell the battle was over and the victory achieved. "It is said that, the royal baggage not having arrived, Philip was unprovided with a bed. 'You shall have the most glorious bed,' cried Vendôme, 'that ever monarch slept on;' and so saying he ordered the standards taken in the battle to be brought together and spread upon the ground for a couch."*

Before day dawned Staremberg and his broken army were retreating with all possible speed, and a few weeks later the Archduke Charles, "who so lately seemed triumphant

* Lord Mahon.

DUC DE VENDÔME

Sovereign of Spain, found his possession in it scarcely extend beyond the two sea fortresses of Tarragona and Barcelona."*

How far did the Princess des Ursins' exertions contribute to bring about this sudden change of affairs, a change which at last established Philip V. securely on the throne of Spain? "If her courage had wavered after the defeat of Saragossa," writes François Combes, "if she had not had confidence in the ultimate success of the Spaniards into whose hands she had confided the fate of the King, . . . and if finally she had not set an example of firmness to Louis XIV. himself, which that monarch felt bound at last to imitate, there is no doubt whatever that Philip V. would have lost Spain, and with it the Indies." But Madame des Ursins had steadily pursued her course unshaken by defeats and unmoved by bribes or threats from Versailles. "Thus it is," he observes, "that events can be moulded beforehand by persons of character and resolution."

* Lord Mahon.

CHAPTER XV

A WILY PRIEST

THE long wars of the Spanish Succession were now drawing to a close. The Allies had become convinced by their complete defeat at Villaviciosa that further efforts in favour of the Archduke would be vain, seeing that Spain had declared unreservedly for Philip V. And soon afterwards an event occurred to cause them no longer even to wish to see the Archduke on the throne of Spain. His elder brother, the Emperor Joseph, died, leaving no son to succeed him, and the Austrian crown, with all its dependencies, therefore, devolved upon the Archduke Charles. The English and Dutch now considered that it "was just as important to guard against the union of the Spanish dominions with those of Austria as with those of France." In the meanwhile a change of Ministry in England had dismissed the Whigs, the promoters of the war, from power, and had brought in the Tories, who eagerly desired peace. Negotiations were commenced early in 1712.

There was no longer any question, among the contending parties, of Philip V. abandoning the throne of Spain. His position had become unassailable. The King was well aware to whom he mainly owed his success, and he showed some appreciation of Madame des Ursins' services by conferring upon her a rank equal to that of the princesses of the blood royal. At this juncture of affairs Madame des Ursins committed a fault, in policy at least, for which she has been much blamed. She desired Philip to endow her with a small principality in the Netherlands, which she wished afterwards to exchange for part of the province of Touraine, in France. The province, at her death, was to revert to its lawful Sovereign. The request does not seem to be unreasonable. Madame des Ursins had experienced strange vicissitudes of fortune, and she knew that royal favour could not be relied upon. She desired, therefore, to secure for herself a retreat where she might enjoy peace and independence for the remainder of her advanced life. But her project was regarded with a jealous eye at Versailles. At that Court her desire for sovereignty, though on so small a scale and for so limited a period, was looked upon as an act of gross presumption. Not only was it disapproved of by her active enemies of the Orleanist faction, but even by some of her friends, and much opposition had to be encountered. The very difficulties in its way seemed to sharpen Madame des Ursins' desire to obtain her object, and she continued its pursuit when it would have been wiser to have abandonded it. So confident was she of ultimate success, that she purchased the manor of Chanteloup in the neighbourhood of Tours, and made arrangements for the erection of a mansion which she hoped soon to occupy.

The claims of the Princess des Ursins were discussed at the Peace Congress at Utrecht, and they caused some delay in its proceedings. At last on April 11, 1713, a treaty of peace was finally concluded, but the article concerning Madame des Ursins' principality was left out. She failed to obtain her desired retreat, but her long and gallant championship of Philip V. had not been carried on for personal ends. Amelot, writing to Louis XIV. in the troubled year of 1709, remarks : " The Princess des Ursins is so disinterested that she does not receive either her salaries or pensions, simply because she does not ask for them. She even does good to those whom she knows to be her enemies." The true reward of Madame des Ursins' work in Spain was obtained when she saw Philip V. firmly established on his throne, and the Bourbon dynasty acknowledged by the whole of Europe. It is true that there was some division of the vast possessions of the Spanish crown, but, in retaining Spain and the Indies, Philip kept by far the most important portion.

After the conclusion of peace the Princess des Ursins inaugurated several changes in the Constitution and Government of Spain. Some of these tended too much to exalt the power of the Sovereign and to depress that of the nobles; some, however, were wise and just reforms. One of the latter affected the finances. A "formless and confused system" of ancient standing was replaced by the most enlightened system of that day.

Another wise reform had reference to the Inquisition. We have seen how, in the early part of her career as Camarera-Mayor, Madame des Ursins withstood that power. She now renewed the contest. Not because the Inquisition was opposed to Philip's rule, for, on the contrary, it claimed to be his staunch supporter and used its grim weapons in his defence, but Madame des Ursins abhorred those weapons and desired no help from such an ally. She endeavoured to arouse public opinion against the proceedings of the Inquisition, but unfortunately the nation still regarded it as an integral part of their religion and therefore stood aloof. Her brave contest, however, did not fail to produce good results. "Through her active intervention," writes

Geffroy, 'a request of the English Government was granted that the residence of their Ambassador at Madrid should form a legal refuge for all persons pursued by the emissaries of the Inquisition. Thus," he continues, "a Protestant nation set up in the very capital of the Catholic King a permanent place of shelter from the cruel acts of the Holy Office. It was a remarkable innovation, and was the first blow struck by the spirit of modern thought against the old institutions of Spain, which were the outcome of the superstitious and often barbarous religion of the Middle Ages." A further concession was made by which British ships lying in Spanish ports should also become refuges for the victims of religious persecution.

The rulers of the Inquisition, who well knew that "terror formed the basis of its power and universal submission its prestige," saw that a breach had been made in its stronghold, that might never be repaired. Anger and fear alike produced a secret determination among them to compass the downfall of their enemy, "the audacious Frenchwoman who was the cause of all their trouble."*

In the commencement of the year 1714 sorrow fell upon the Court of Madrid through the death of the young queen after a lingering illness. Her loss was deeply mourned by the nation, for her undaunted courage under severe trials and her affectionate and unselfish nature had greatly endeared her to the Spaniards. St. Simon, who visited Spain seven years later, writes: "All classes, whether nobles, military men, or common people, still regard their loss as irreparable, and dwell upon it, even now, with tears." Philip, who had always been much attached to his wife, was almost crushed by her death. He could not face the thought of reigning without her by his side and talked of abdicating in favour of the Prince of Asturias, a child only six years old. Madame des Ursins alone could induce him to listen to counsels of reason. She reminded him of the courage and resignation recently shown by the King of France when death had suddenly cut off the

* François Combes.

flower of his family in the persons of the Duke and Duchess of Burgundy and their eldest son the Duke of Brittany. All the hopes of Louis XIV. for a direct successor to his throne now centred upon a sickly child of three years of age. Yet the old King bore up bravely and continued to rule the affairs of his State. Philip's courage was aroused, and he abandoned the idea of abdication.

The Queen had left three young children. At Philip's earnest request, the Princess des Ursins assumed the office of their "gouvernante." From this period her position at Court was beset with difficulties. Philip, melancholy and indolent, leant more and more upon her for counsel and help, thus exposing her to constant jealousy and ill-will. The situation of affairs at the palace was eagerly discussed in the salons of both Madrid and Paris, and St. Simon, who never fails to record the gossip of the day, relates the following anecdote. Philip, he tells us, had retired one evening with his confessor, Père Robinet, into the recess of a window in order to converse privately. Robinet, wishing to excite the King's curiosity, assumed an air of constraint and mystery which naturally provoked a question as to its cause. He then replied that since his Majesty commanded him to speak openly he felt bound to tell him that no one, either in France or Spain, doubted that he intended to marry the Princess des Ursins. "*I* marry her!" exclaimed the King, "no, indeed!" The story recalls the former words of the Princess herself, when accused by the Abbé d'Estrée of being married to d'Aubigny. "Pour mariée, non!"

Philip was annoyed by this idle gossip, though affecting to despise it. To cut it short he requested Madame des Ursins to select a new Queen for him. It was an important commission, and its result would materially affect her own future, as well as that of the King. Her loss in the late Queen was irreparable. It was the loss of a warm friend and a staunch supporter. Where could she find such another woman?

There happened to be in Madrid at this time an Italian priest, a native of the Duchy of

Parma, whose name, hitherto unknown, soon became famous, the Abbé Alberoni. He was ambitious and insinuating. He had managed to attract the grandees to his entertainments, in spite of their dislike of foreigners, by means of his "*séductions culinaires.*" His feasts were celebrated for their dainty Italian dishes and Italian wines. In Alberoni's letters to his friend Rocca, Prime Minister to the Duke of Parma, we find reiterated requests for the despatch of Parmesan cheese, sausages, confectionery, fruits and wines, amidst grave discourses on political events. When the Abbé discovered that a second marriage for Philip V. was under consideration he formed a scheme for advancing the interests of the Duchy of Parma and at the same time for securing his own fortune. Its object was the marriage of the King with Elizabeth Farnese, a niece of the Duke of Parma. Alberoni began at once to gather up and to weave the various threads of his plot. He had always paid especial court to Cardinal Giudici, the Grand Inquisitor. He now went to visit him at Bayonne, where the Cardinal was in a condition of semi-banishment. The Abbé told him that he had a project in hand which would ward off all the dangers that threatened the Inquisition and would restore him, Giudici, to his former position of eminence. Having unfolded his plan, the Abbé remarked that the lady in question was of a high spirited and determined character, little likely to be influenced by the Princess des Ursins, and she it was who might be looked to as the instrument for reinstating the Inquisition in its former position of absolute power. Cardinal Giudici eagerly caught at the suggestion and promised to speak in favour of the match to Louis XIV.

Alberoni next paid his court to Madame des Ursins. His manners were open and sincere, and, accustomed though she was by long habit to detect falsehood and double dealing, she felt in this case perfectly secure. "On peut être plus fin qu'un autre, mais pas plus fin que tous les autres," as the great French moralist has remarked. The priest and the lady entered one day into conversation on the subject of the choice of a new Queen. The wily Italian, well knowing the qualities that Madame des Ursins would look for, observed, "You must find a lady who is quiet and docile, and not likely to interfere in State affairs." "Where shall we discover such a person?" asked his companion. Alberoni ran through the royal families of Europe, and then, as if by accident, carelessly mentioned Elizabeth Farnese, daughter of the late Duke of Parma, adding, with the same tone of simplicity and indifference, "She is a good girl, plump, healthy, and well bred, brought up in the petty Court of her uncle Duke Francis, and accustomed to hear of nothing but needlework and embroidery. You would find no difficulty," he added, "in making her manners assume the proper Spanish gravity and, by keeping her retired from society, as you could naturally do in the capacity of her Camarera-Mayor, you would soon acquire the same influence over her as over her predecessor."* Alberoni did not fail to add a hint of the political advantages of the match. The Princess Elizabeth had reversionary claims

* San Phélipe, also Coxe.

to the Duchies of Parma and of Tuscany, which might afford a means, hereafter, of regaining the Spanish power in Italy. Whilst the Abbé was using these arguments to the Princess des Ursins we find him remarking in a letter to his friend Rocca, "Mais diable! Louanges et grâces á Dieu! It is we (natives of Parma) who are the gainers in this affair."

Madame des Ursins advised Phillip to demand the hand of the Princess Elizabeth, and Alberoni was himself sent to the Duke of Parma to negotiate the marriage. His mission was successful. The Duke readily gave his consent to so splendid a match for his niece, and Alberoni, in return for his services, was endowed with a title of nobility and sent back to Madrid in the capacity of Ambassador of the Court of Parma.

CHAPTER XVI

A KING'S GRATITUDE

MADAME DES URSINS, in the midst of her fancied security, had a sudden suspicion that all might not be right. It is true she had been duly appointed by Philip Camarera-Mayor to the Queen-elect of Spain, but she had written twice to that lady and had received no answer. Was is possible that Alberoni had deceived her respecting the character of Elizabeth Farnese? She had an interview with the Abbé at once and questioned him closely, taking care, at the same time, to betray no sign of uneasiness. Alberoni replied to her questions with his usual air of openness and bonhomie. There seemed to be no cause for alarm. Still Madame des Ursins did not feel satisfied. She made inquiries in other quarters, and her suspicions were so far confirmed as to determine her to postpone the marriage. The ceremony was to take place on August 16 at Parma by proxy. Madame des Ursins, who represented the Court of Madrid in the various arrangements, despatched a trusty messenger on August 8 with a commission to stop the proceedings. But her opponents were as vigilant as herself. Arrived at the Court of Parma, her messenger was either thrown into prison or bribed to keep silence. The marriage took place and the new wife of Philip V. commenced her journey to Spain.

In spite of the failure of her efforts to delay the marriage, Madame des Ursins had cause to feel somewhat reassured as the new Queen ratified her appointment as Camarera-Mayor. But her anxiety, though lessened, was by no means removed. The future was wrapped in ominous clouds. Still "ever mistress of herself" through every phase of fortune, she gave her mind, to the last, to the interests of Spain. "She assisted the Duke d'Escalone in founding an Academy of the Spanish language formed in imitation of the Académie Française."* This noble institution was established while Elizabeth Farnese was making her journey towards Spain, and when the train that was laid in the path of the Camarera-Mayor was about to explode."

Alberoni had, for long past, been preparing the catastrophe, as is now proved by his published letters.† He had instilled jealousy of Madame des Ursins' influence into the mind of the new Queen, and had done all in his power to make her think ill of her Camarera-Mayor, whom he describes as "the most knavish woman in the world." The poison worked, and one day Philip V. received a private letter from his bride-elect to the following effect: "I only make one demand, and that is the dismissal of Madame des Ursins. Give me full powers in this matter. My happiness in my Court will depend upon the issue." And what did the King reply? He feared to offend the Queen, and he feared yet more to provoke the resentment of the Inquisition if he espoused the cause

* François Combes.
† "Lettres Intimes de J. M. Alberoni," publiées par Emile Bourgeois.

of Madame des Ursins. He, therefore, gave Elizabeth *carte blanche* to act as she chose, and basely delivered his staunch friend to her mercy.

The new Queen halted on her journey through the south of France at St. Jean-Pied-de-Port, where she was the guest of her aunt the Queen-Dowager of Spain, who was a close ally of the Grand Inquisitor and of Alberoni. Here the plot for the fall of the Princess des Ursins was conceived, but it was matured at Pampeluna, where the Queen was met by Alberoni himself. There every detail was settled, and every precaution taken for the success of the scheme. The meeting between the Queen and the Princess des Ursins was to take place at Guadraque, a small village in advance of Guadalaxara, where the King and Court were to await her arrival. Alberoni arranged that whilst the interview was taking place he would stand outside the door of the Queen's apartment talking with apparent carelessness to two officers of the guard, whom he could trust to support his action. Meanwhile the attendants of the Princess were to be secured to prevent their rendering her assistance, and the high road to Guadalaxara was to be guarded so that she could not despatch a messenger to the King or to her friends at Court. Finally the master of the village inn was to be forbidden to provide her with post horses.

Alberoni drafted two letters in the Queen's name, which she copied out in her own handwriting and put aside to be used at the right moment. One was an order to the captain of the guard to carry out the military measures necessary for the success of their conspiracy, the other was a letter of explanation to the King to be despatched after the blow had been struck.*

The King and Court left Madrid on December 19 (1714). "Three hours before her departure the Princess des Ursins' salons were thronged with nobles and State dignitaries of all ranks, who formed a Court equal in numbers and distinction to that of the King himself. . . . The new Queen had allowed her

* See Armstrong's "Elizabeth Farnese."

to retain her position of Camarera-Mayor. That fact was sufficient for the courtiers, who doubted not that in personal intercourse with her Majesty, Madame des Ursins' genius would again ensure her dominance. Their expectations were confirmed by her exultant bearing, both on receiving their compliments and good wishes, and on returning from her audience with the King, an audience which was to be her last."*

"On the 22nd December," writes St. Simon, "the King of Spain reached Guadalaxara. The following morning, the 23rd, the Princess des Ursins, accompanied by a very few attendants, proceeded seven leagues farther on the road, to a small village called Guadraqué, where the bridal train was to halt that night. On reaching Guadraqué she found that the Queen had already arrived. She alighted at a lodging prepared for her close to that of the royal traveller. Madame des Ursins was in full Court costume, richly jewelled. Having paused a few minutes to adjust her attire, she was

* Geffroy.

ushered into the Queen's presence. The coldness of her reception surprised her extremely, but she attributed it to natural embarrassment, and endeavoured to thaw the lady's icy reserve. Meanwhile the company who were present gradually dispersed, and the two were left alone.

"Conversation now began, but the Queen abruptly put a stop to it by angrily reproaching the Princess for venturing to come into her presence in festival costume, and with manners that were disrespectful. Madame des Ursins, whose dress was in strict accordance with Spanish etiquette, and whose courteous demeanour might well have restored the Queen to a right mind, was astounded. She attempted to reply to these charges, but the Queen broke out into vehement abuse, and then called loudly for the officers of her escort to come to her assistance. Again Madame des Ursins attempted to speak, but the Queen's fury was redoubled. 'Turn out this mad woman,' she cried, and seeing them hesitate, she herself pushed her guest out by the shoulders."

The Queen then gave orders for the immediate arrest of the Princess des Ursins, and commanded that she should forthwith be placed in a travelling coach and six, and sent off with all speed under a guard of soldiers to the Spanish frontier. "When Amenzaga, the officer in command, ventured to inform her that the King of Spain alone possessed the right to give such an order, she asked him haughtily if he had not received instructions from the King to yield her implicit and unquestioning obedience? He could not deny that he had received such instructions, but to what they tended he had had no conception.

"The Princess des Ursins was therefore arrested. She was allowed no time to change her dress nor to take any precautions against the cold. She had neither money nor food for the journey. One of her female attendants only was permitted to accompany her. She was hurried into her State carriage· wearing her magnificent attire just as she had quitted the presence of the Queen. Two officers were on horseback ready to accompany her, together with a guard of fifty dragoons. It was nearly seven o'clock in the evening. The ground was covered with snow. The cold was intense, so intense that the coachman's hand was frostbitten. Black darkness prevailed, save for the faint light afforded by the glimmering snow. Under such conditions the Princess des Ursins was borne onwards, whilst the long winter night gradually wore away. When morning dawned it was necessary to halt in order to bait the horses. But for human beings there was no decent food to be obtained."

At each halting-place Madame des Ursins expected to find a messenger from the King of Spain bearing a letter of apology and explanation, and expressing a desire for her return to Madrid. But no such messenger appeared, and "in proportion as she journeyed further and further away as time ran on and no information reached her, she gradually realised that all hope of succour was vain. . . . The Princess, who had now attained the age of seventy years, had no rest, no proper food, nor even a change of clothes for twenty-three days, at the end of which time she reached the border town of St. Jean-de-Luz." Here what vivid recollections must have assailed her of her triumphal entry into Spain at the same place ten years before! The contrast between her condition then and now must indeed have added poignancy to her mental sufferings. " But Madame des Ursins was true to herself. Neither tears, regrets, reproaches, nor the slightest irritability escaped her. The two officers who guarded her were struck with admiration at such self-control."

At St. Jean-de-Luz her physical sufferings ceased, and she regained her liberty, for here her military escort left her. Here also she found friends. Her two nephews Messrs. Lanti and Chalais, who were in Madrid at the time of her disgrace, had requested permission of Philip V. to join their aunt at St. Jean-de-Luz. Their request was granted, and the King made use of the occasion to send her a final communication by their hands. The long-expected letter was therefore at last delivered to Madame des Ursins. But what did it contain? A few polite expressions of concern at what had

A CHAMPION'S RECOMPENSE

occurred, and of regret at "his inability to oppose his authority to the wishes of his Queen."

It was well for Madame des Ursins that her brilliant successes had never blinded her eyes to the nature of Court favour. When she first entered Spain with the royal couple in the autumn of 1701, she wrote to Madame de Maintenon : " I hardly know which of their Majesties seems to honour and love me most. I should feel greatly flattered if I could but forget the fact that Kings are made to *be* loved, but that they in their hearts love no one."

CHAPTER XVII

PEACE AFTER STORM

THE Princess des Ursins wrote to Louis XIV., to Torcy, to Villeroy, and to Madame de Maintenon, informing them of the extraordinary treatment she had received. She writes to the latter: "I await the King's [of France] orders at St. Jean-de-Luz where I am staying in a small house by the sea shore. I see the ocean often stormy — sometimes calm. Such is the life of Courts, such has been my own life. . . . I do indeed hold with you that we must look for stability in God alone. Certainly it is not to be found in the hearts of men, for who could have felt more secure than I did of the friendship of the King of Spain?"

Once more she requested permission to make her appearance before the King to vindicate her conduct. The permission was granted. Madame de Maintenon wrote in reply: "Be assured that I shall not fail you. My affection for you has not been won by the public personage whom I admire, but by the woman whom I esteem."

Madame des Ursins reached Versailles in the month of March (1715). She still hoped to retrieve her fortunes. But Versailles was no longer the Versailles of ten years ago. The old King's reign was drawing to a close, and the whole Court was at the feet of the Duke of Orleans, the Regent that was to be. What favour could be expected for the person who had discovered and exposed his treasonable conduct in Spain? Even St. Simon, who had formerly boasted of his intimacy with the "dictatress of the Court," now humbly applied to the Duke for permission to visit her. He was in a ludicrous dilemma, desiring to satisfy his curiosity as a chronicler, but by no means to injure his position as a friend of the man who would soon be all-powerful. "We came to a compromise," he naïvely remarks. "The

Duke and Duchess of Orleans gave me leave to visit the Princess des Ursins twice—once at Versailles, and once here (in Paris) before she left. But I promised not to see her a third time, and I engaged that Madame de St. Simon should not visit her at all. This last condition was hard to swallow, but there was no help for it." St. Simon gives us a detailed account of his conversations with the Princess, whom he found brave and cheerful as ever, and ready to recount the particulars of her downfall as if they related to another person. Their first interview lasted eight hours. "One can easily imagine," he writes, "what a number of subjects passed under review in such a long tête-à-tête. She predicted many things which have since come to pass. Those eight hours, enriched by her curious and varied discourse, flew by like eight seconds."

The Duke of Orleans' whims and caprices were now regarded as laws. Louis XIV. himself felt bound to make concessions respecting his intercourse with the Princess des Ursins, and, in accordance with the Duke's desire, requested her not to appear at any social gathering that was attended by a member of the Orleans family. This prohibition greatly restricted her visits to the palace. But in her brother Mons. de Noirmoutier's house, in Paris, she had the comfort of intercourse with some of her oldest friends, such as the Maréchale de Noailles and Marshal Villeroy. She was glad to be again at times with Madame de Maintenon, but that lady was now in constant attendance upon the old King, whose strength was rapidly failing.

The alarming condition of the King's health determined Madame des Ursins to quit France without loss of time, for she knew that she could not count even upon personal liberty in a country governed by the Duke of Orleans. She left Paris on August 14, accompanied by her two nephews, and made all speed to reach the frontiers of Savoy. Just before she arrived at Chambéry she received intelligence of the death of the King. " We must bow beneath the hand that strikes us," wrote Madame de Maintenon from Saint Cyr, where she had promptly retired; "I wish your condition were as blessed as mine. I have seen the King die like a saint and a hero. I have left the world which I never loved, and I am established in a calm and peaceful retreat." Madame des Ursins responds by expressing her own admiration for the King's "noble death," and then adds, "For myself, I know not where I shall be allowed to die."

The political career of the Princess des Ursins was ended. In one of her letters, written after her fall, she declares that the main objects of her policy had been to place Philip V. firmly on his throne, and to promote a friendly union between the great nations of France and Spain for their mutual benefit. "We fully believe this," writes François Combes. "The statement is confirmed by all her public acts. But to these lofty aims she added another—a desire to institute reforms in Spain for which the country was not yet ready." "In our opinion," observes the Marquis de San Phélipe, "the storm which tore down Madame des Ursins had its origin at St. Jean-Pied-de-Port."

Now the same historian declares that the Grand Inquisitor was the hidden life and soul of the famous interview which there took place. Setting aside, therefore, some minor circumstances which hastened the catastrophe, "Madame des Ursins fell a victim to her contest with the Inquisition—a contest which, though an error in policy, was a noble error, and one which, in the eyes of many, will confer upon her a lasting title to fame."

As soon as the Princess des Ursins was out of the way Philip gave his consent to the Inquisition being reinstated in all its former power, and made Cardinal del Giudici, the Grand Inquisitor, Minister for Foreign Affairs. The wily Alberoni also managed to secure for himself a post of importance. There was a general retrograde movement in Spain, brought about largely by the new Queen and her supporters. Many wise reforms were abolished, and the old laws and customs of the Austro-Spanish rule re-established. Frederick the Great said of Elizabeth Farnese that "Spartan pride, English obstinacy, Italian finesse, and

French vivacity made up the character of this singular woman. She proceeded with an audacious directness to the accomplishment of her designs. Nothing could change her course, nothing could stop her." Carlyle has called her "the Termagant of Spain." It is curious to turn to Alberoni's letters, written after his triumph, and to see the thraldom under which he lived. The Queen was an ardent huntress, and she pursued the sport at all seasons and in all weathers. The Abbé was expected to accompany her, and he had to spend many hours in the depth of winter in the snowy mountains of the Guadarrama, standing by the side of his mistress, loading her guns and handing them to her. No wonder that he exclaims to his confidant, in the bitterness of his spirit, "I had rather be a galley slave to the Grand Turk! I only wish that those who envy me could be in my place for a single day!"

Madame des Ursins took up her residence at Genoa. She writes from St. Pierre-d'Arène to her nephew, just a year after her fall: "I am enjoying a privacy and solitude such as I have not known for many years, and which certainly has its advantages. I now begin to feel that there is no blessing in this world equal to repose. . . . The wise will neither be uplifted nor cast down by the changes of fortune. Time is the great master of all things, and whatever troubles may arise we should never esteem ourselves unhappy if we are guiltless of having produced them ourselves."

Two years later Philip V., who perhaps felt at last some compunction for his treatment of her, sent the Princess des Ursins a friendly message by his Ambassador at Genoa, the historian San Phélipe. She writes to her friend Orry, who had shared her disgrace (Genoa, April 25, 1718): "The King of Spain has done me the honour to assure me by the mouth of the Marquis de San Phélipe, whom he sent to me for this purpose, that he will continue to bestow upon me his esteem, his friendship, and his protection; and that in whatever countries I may choose to sojourn, his Ambassadors will be ordered to act in accordance with these sentiments."

At the same time Philip accorded her a pension. Madame des Ursins was gratified by these tokens of returning favour, and the assurances respecting the conduct of Philip's Ambassadors enabled her to carry out a cherished wish of spending the remainder of her life in Rome.

In the meanwhile strange changes had taken place in Spain, where Alberoni had caused a war to break out with France. When the Quadruple Alliance put an end to this war Alberoni's ascendancy also came to an end, and he quitted Madrid, but not before he had succeeded in ousting the Grand Inquisitor, Cardinal Giudici, from power.

When, in the year 1719, the Princess des Ursins took up her residence in Rome, whom should she find there but her old enemies Alberoni and Giudici! The three exiles met in that city, the resort "*des grandeurs déchues et des disgraces décentes.*"

"The Princess was received in Rome," writes St. Simon, "with every mark of respect by the Pope and his Court, by the Sacred College, and by all the leading personages, and she was welcomed by the Court of the exiled Stuarts, having been formerly on terms of friendship with the ex-Queen Mary of Modena.

On December 5, 1722, the Princess des Ursins died. She had reached the advanced age of eighty, but "was still fresh complexioned, upright, graceful and attractive, and her mind was as clear and vigorous as ever."* "One of the most original and distinctive features of Madame des Ursins' character," remarks Ste. Beuve, "was her tranquillity of mind in the midst of so active and stormy a career, and it was this tranquillity which enabled her, after her terrible fall, to live peacefully in retirement and to die of old age at eighty." Her letters unfold her character. They are the true reflection of her mind in its varying moods. "Her style," writes Geffroy, "is delightfully playful when she is dealing with social or domestic life, polished and graceful when she is soliciting or bestowing favours, incisive, ardent, impassioned when she is in the crisis of a contest, firm and

* St. Simon.

imperious when she commands, solemn in triumph, and calm, dignified, and reticent in defeat."

St. Simon, who was often unjust in his estimate of Madame des Ursins' motives and conduct, was, nevertheless, strongly impressed by her character. "She was," he remarks, "an extraordinary personage throughout the whole course of her long life, one who figured in a grand and exceptional manner, one whose courage, perseverance, and powers of resource were most rare. Her rule in Spain was so absolute and so widely recognised, and her character of so unique a combination of qualities, that her life deserves to be written, and to take its place as one of the most curious chapters in the history of her times."

So writes a contemporary historian, and more than a hundred years later the verdict of posterity is thus recorded by Geffroy: "A reaction followed the fall of the Princess des Ursins, but the fruit of her labours has not perished. In contributing largely to prevent the wreck, at one time so imminent, of the

Bourbon dynasty in Spain, she laid the foundation of all modern reforms in that country. The history of her life is the first page of the history of Spain in the eighteenth century."

INDEX

ABRANTÉS, Duc d', 2-3

Aix, Archbishop of, interviews with Louis XIV. respecting Princess des Ursins, 62-3

Alberoni, Abbé (afterwards Cardinal), his banquets, 216-17 ; forms scheme for marriage of Philip V. with Elizabeth Farnese and wins approval of Cardinal Giudici and of Princess des Ursins, 217-20 ; is sent to negotiate marriage, 220 ; made Ambassador to Court of Parma, 220 ; instils jealousy of Princess des Ursins' influence into mind of new Queen, 223 ; meets Queen at Pampeluna, 224 ; arranges plot for downfall of Princess des Ursins, 224-5 ; secures post of importance, 237 ; thraldom under Elizabeth Farnese, 238 ; ascendancy in Spain ends; ousts Cardinal Giudici and retires to Rome, 240

Alcantara, loss of, 100-1

Allies proclaim Archduke as Charles III. King of Spain, 60 ; victories of, in Netherlands, 102 ; causes of division in camp, 120-1 ; defeated at battle of Almanza, 141-2 ; their terms of peace harsh, 181-2 ; negotiations with Duke of Orleans, 183 ; victory of Saragossa, 196-7 ; re-enter Madrid, 200-1 ; defeated at Villaviciosa, 208 ; change of views, 208-9

Almanza, battle of, 141-2 ; results of, 146

Alva, Duke of, 66, 90-1

Alva, Duchess of, 66

Amelot, Marquis de Gournay, at Canillas, 82 ; appointed French Ambassador, 86, 87, 88, 97 ; advises Queen's retreat to Burgos, 105 ; letter to Louis XIV., 149 ; 171, 174 ; resigns his post, 182 ; testimony in favour of Princess des Ursins, 211

Amenzaga, 228

Anjou, Duke of. See Philip V.

Aragon, Province of, hails Archduke as King of Spain, 93 ; Philip V. retreats through, 100 ; subjection of, 146 ; deprived of privileges, 147, 184-5

Arcos, Duc d', 177

INDEX

Asturias, Prince of, preparations for birth of, 137-8, 150-3; description of, 154-5; oath of allegiance to, 180; flight from Madrid, 200, 214
Atocha, Church of the Virgin of, State ceremonies at, 123-4, 135-7
Aubigny, Le Sieur d', 44-6, 157
Auto-da-fé, description of, by eye-witness, 21-4

BARCELONA, inhabitants of, welcome Archduke as King of Spain, 93; siege of, 98-9
Benevente, Count de, 15
Berlanga, Queen halts at, 105, 108
Berwick, Duke of, 51; Generalissimo in Spain, 92; praised by Princess des Ursins, 101; advises the Queen to retreat to Burgos, 103-5; unable to defend Madrid, 104; remarks on campaign of 1706, 124-5, 138; is provided with means to pay soldiers, 140-1; gains battle of Almanza, 141-2; conquers Valencia and Aragon, his severity, 146; his integrity, created Duke of Liria, 147, 162-3; is withdrawn from Spain, 164
Besons, Marshal, commands French troops in Spain, 181; treacherous conduct of, 187-90; is withdrawn, 190
Blécourt, French Chargé-d'affaires, 2-3
Bourbon, House of, emblem of, 99
Bracciano, Duc de. See Prince Orsini
Bragelonne, Chevalier, 104, 107
Brihuega, defeat of General Stanhope at, 205
Brittany, Duke of, birth of, 154; death of, 215
Buen Retiro, palace of, arrival of nurses at, 150-2; grounds improved by Princess des Ursins, 160-1
Burgos, Court removes to, 104-5; Court leaves, 122
Burgundy, Duke of, 144; commands army in Flanders, 166; death of, 215
Burgundy, Duchess of, 4, 68, 84, 111, 154; death of, 215
Burke, Colonel, 40

CABARON, Queen halts at, 122-3
Canillas, 82
Carthagena, Governor of, surrenders to the Allies, 116
Carpenter, General, 205
Casa del Cordón, 113
Castel, Rodrigue, 105
Castile, Admiral of (Don Juan Henriquez of Cabrera), joins party of Archduke, 38-41
Castile, poverty of, 109; difficult to subdue, 203-4
Castilians, rally round Philip V., 118-19

INDEX

Catalonia, revolt in, 60; acknowledges Archduke Charles as King of Spain, 93
Chalais, Prince de, 7
Chalais, M. de, 230
Chambéry, arrival of Princess des Ursins at, 235
Chamillart, Marquis de, 97, 138; brings news of victory of Almanza to Louis XIV., 143, 144, 181
Chanteloup, manor of, 210
Charles II., King of Spain, death of, 1; his Will, 1-3; witnesses an auto-da-fé in 1680, 22-4; household of, 27; reasons for appointing Philip V. as his successor, 94-5
Charles, Archduke of Austria, claimant to throne of Spain, 2, 30; is acknowledged King of Spain by King of Portugal, 41; is proclaimed King of Spain by Allies, under title of Charles III., 60; is welcomed by the Catalonians, 93; is proclaimed by the Allies King of Spain and Overlord of the Netherlands, 102; recognised as Charles III. of Spain by the Pope, 102; is proclaimed King in Madrid, 115; his portrait, 120; postpones triumphal entry into Madrid, 121; satirical medal, 140; withdraws Spanish contingent to Catalonia, 142; learns of his defeat at Almanza, 145-6; enters Saragossa in triumph, acknowledged King throughout Aragon, 197; enters Madrid in triumph, 201; tries in vain to gain new adherents, 201-2; is forced to retire from Madrid, witnesses joy of inhabitants at his departure, 203-4; defeat at Villaviciosa, 205-7; Tarragona and Barcelona the only possessions left him in Spain, 207; succeeds his brother as Emperor of Austria, 208
Chateauneuf, M. de, 58
Churchill, Arabella, 92
Coulanges, Madame de, 10-11
Court of Spain, reforms in, 27-9; is removed to Burgos, 104-5, 110, 126-7; is removed to Valladolid, 200-1

Das Minas, triumphant entry of, into Madrid, 104
Dauphin, Monsr. le, 144
Diaz, Friolan, victim of Inquisition, 33-5

Egmont, Duchesse d', 66
Escalone, Duc d', 222-3
Estrée, Abbé d', replaces Cardinal d'Estrée as Ambassador at Madrid, 44; affair of mutilated despatch, 45-6, 49; letter to, from Louis XIV 50-1
Estrée, Cardinal d', head of ultra-French party, 43; is recalled, 44
Eugène, Prince, 166

INDEX

FAGON, Court physician at Versailles, 159

Farnese, Elizabeth, is proposed by Alberoni as second wife for Philip V., and approved by Cardinal Giudici, 217-18; by Princess des Ursins, 218-20; her hand is demanded by Philip, 220; married by proxy at Parma, commences journey to Spain, 222; writes to Philip demanding dismissal of Princess des Ursins, 223; halts on journey at St. Jean-Pied-de-Port, is guest of Queen-Dowager of Spain, meets Alberoni at Pampeluna, 224; they arrange plot for downfall of Princess des Ursins, 224-5; meets Princess des Ursins at Guadraqué, 226; their interview; orders her arrest, 227-8; character of, by Frederick the Great, 237-8; "Termagant of Spain," 238

Figueras, 13, 14

Fleet, English, off Vigo, 37-8; relieves Barcelona, 99

Flotte, M., agent of the Duke of Orleans, 183-4; is arrested, 185

French language, modern, modelled, 89-90

Frias, Duke de, High Constable of Castile, made Major-domo-Major, 91-2

GALWAY, Earl of (Marquis de Ruvigny), triumphant entry into Madrid, 104; commands allied forces at battle of Almanza, 141

Gazette de France, 153

Gibraltar, lost to Spain, 60, 92

Giudici, Cardinal (Grand Inquisitor), Alberoni pays court to, 217-18; plans fall of Princess des Ursins, 224, 237; appointed Minister of Foreign Affairs, 237; is ousted from power, retires to Rome, 240

Grammont, Duc de, sent as Ambassador to Madrid, his secret mission, 55; meets Princess des Ursins at Vittoria, 56; interview with the Queen, 57; his despatches, 58-9; curious correspondence with Louis XIV., 74-6; failure of mission, 76; resigns his post, 86

Grand Alliance formed, 29

Grandees, loyalty of, to Philip V., 177-9, 200-2; petition Louis XIV. to send Vendôme as Generalissimo to Spain, 203; zeal at battle of Villaviciosa, 206

Guadalaxara, 224-5

Guadraqué, 224; meeting of Elizabeth Farnese and Princess des Ursins at, 226

HARCOURT, Duc d', 5, 24-5, 63, 67-8

Harrach, Count d', 2, 3

Höchstet (Blenheim) battle of, 95

Hostelnuovo, 13

INQUISITION, the, 21, 23; opposition to, by Princess des Ursins, 33-5; English Ambassador's house and English ships made refuges for

INDEX

victims of, 212-13 ; rulers of, determine to compass downfall of Princess des Ursins, 213-14, 218 ; is reinstated in its former power, 237

Italy, campaigns in, 30, 102

JAMES II., 29, 92
James Francis Edward, Prince. See Pretender
Jansenists and Jesuists, 161
Joseph, Emperor, death of, 208

KING of Spain. See Philip V.

LABOURDONNAY, Governor of Bordeaux, 107
Lanti, M., 230
Lerma, Queen halts at, 108
Liganez, Marquis de, arrested, 87-8
Lille, captured by the Allies, 167
Lisbon, Treaty of, 41
Louis XIV. bids farewell to his grandson Philip V. of Spain, 4 ; chooses a wife for him, 4 ; letter declaring choice of Princess des Ursins as Camarera-Mayor, 5-6 ; describes character of Philip V., 25 ; recognises the Pretender as James III. of England, 29 ; advice concerning treasure-ships, 36 ; adopts plan of Princess des Ursins, 37 ; recalls Cardinal d'Estrée, 44 ; receives mutilated dispatch, 46-7 ; resolves to recall Princess des Ursins, 47 ; letters on this subject, 47-9 ; sends order of banishment, 51 ; takes measures to prevent her return to power, 57-8 ; grants leave for private audience, 63 ; *tête-à-tête* with Princess des Ursins, 68 ; his flattering attentions, 69-70 ; at the Marly balls, 71-3 ; secret correspondence with Duc de Grammont on subject of Princess des Ursins, 74-6 ; " treaty " signed at Marly, 79 ; confers honours on Princess des Ursins, 79-80 ; letter in her praise to Queen of Spain, 85 ; suffers defeat in the Netherlands, 102 ; letter to Philip V. on freedom of speech, 128 ; receives news of victory of Almanza, 143-4 ; his love of fresh air, 158-9 ; secret overtures to Allies, concludes Treaty of Milan, 164 ; letter to Philip V. on loss of Lille, 167 ; advises Philip to renounce the kingdoms of Spain and the Indies, 174-5 ; is in treaty with the Allies, 177 ; issues orders for withdrawal of his troops from Spain, consents to leave a few behind, 181 ; threatens to fight with the Allies in the Netherlands against Philip, 181-2 ; rejects the Allies' terms of peace, 182 ; condones treasonable conduct of Duke of Orleans, 185-6 ; and of Marshal Besons, 190 ; renews efforts to induce Philip to accept the Allies' terms of peace, 197-9 ; consents to send Vendôme as Generalissimo to Spain, 202-3 ; resignation under bereavement, 214-15 ; reign drawing to a close, 233 ;

INDEX

concessions to Duke of Orleans, 234-5; strength failing, death, 235

Louville, M. de, 45

MADRID, scene in royal palace of, 1-3; unfit to resist an attack, 98, 104; Queen's flight from, 104; Court returns to, 126; joy on hearing of victory of Almanza, 142; excitement in, 177

Maintenon, Madame de, Françoise d'Aubigné, correspondence with Princess des Ursins, 9; obtains change in sentence of banishment, 60; gains permission for private audience, 63; at the Marly balls, 72-3; "treaty" signed at Marly, 79; letters to Princess des Ursins on the Queen's flight from Madrid, 111, 113; on receiving news of victory of Almanza, 143-4; on domestic and social subjects, 157-9; on terrible condition of France, desires peace at any price, 166-7, 169-70, 190-1; alarmed at Princess des Ursins' financial scheme for France, 171-2; fears to censure Besons' conduct, 190; urges the acceptance of Allies' terms of peace, 191; becomes weary of Princess des Ursins' championship of Philip V., affectation of humility, 193; letter to Princess des Ursins when at St. Jean-de-Luz, 233; letter on death of Louis XIV., 235-6

Mancera, Marquis de, his loyalty to Philip V., 201-2; visited by Philip V., 204-5

Marie Louise of Savoy is chosen as wife for Philip V., 4; married by proxy at Turin, meets Princess des Ursins at Villafranca, 12; first meeting with Philip V., 13-14; pleases the Spaniards, 25-6; discards the "tantillo," 28-9; is created Regent, 30; supports Princess des Ursins in the affair of the mutilated despatch, 46, 49; receives letter from Louis XIV., 47-8; accompanies Princess des Ursins to Alcala, 54; interview with Duc de Grammont, 57; thanks Louis XIV. for his reception of Princess des Ursins, 69; welcomes her at Canillas, 82-3; courage under trials, 101; is advised to quit Madrid, 103; commences journey to Burgos, 104; adds personal ornaments to crown jewels to be sold, 107; halts at Berlanga and Lerma, 105, 108; arrives at Burgos, 110; letter from, to Madame de Maintenon, 110-111; quits Burgos, halts at Cabaron, 122-3; meets Philip V. at Segovia, 123; returns to Madrid, 123-4; heir to throne expected, rejoicings in Madrid, 134-7; gives birth to Prince of Asturias, 153; second flight from Madrid to Valladolid, 200; her death, grief of Spanish nation, 214

Marlborough, Duke of, 92; gains battle of Ramillies, 102; takes Lille, 166

Marly, balls at, 71-3; "treaty" signed at, 79; arrival of news of victory of Almanza at, 143-4

INDEX

Mary of Modena (ex-Queen of England) at the Marly balls, 71, 241
Medina-Cœli, Duke de, 45; made leader of new Ministry, 180; is arrested, 194
Mendoza, Archbishop of Segovia and Grand Inquisitor, 34
Mercure Galant, account of Princess des Ursins' reception in Spain, 81-3
Milan, Treaty of, 164
Millot, Abbé, on French and Spanish character, 31-2
Minorca, island of, lost to Spain, 165
Miquelets, 106
Molière, plays first acted in Spain, 21, 90
Monteillano, Duchess de, 52
Montellano, Conde di, head of the National Party, 33; made President of the Council of Castile, 41

NETHERLANDS, campaign in the, 102
Noailles, Duc de, 28, 102; is sent on confidential mission to Madrid, 197-9
Noailles, Maréchale de, 14, 235
Noirmontier, M. de, brother of Princess des Ursins, created a duke, 80, 235

OLMO, Joseph del, describes an auto-da-fé, 22-4
Orleans, Duke of (afterwards Regent of France), replaces Berwick as Generalissimo in Spain, 168; goes on an embassy to Louis XIV., 168; anger against Princess des Ursins, 173-4; intrigues to obtain the crown of Spain for himself, 183-4; failure of plot, 185-6; party of, 195-6; Court of Versailles at feet of, 233-4
Orleans, Duchess of (mother of the Regent), 132
Orleans, Duchess of, wife of the Regent, 234
Orry, Sieur, 87, 239
Orsini, Prince, and Duc de Boracciano, 5-7; his death, 10 ?

PAMPELUNA, 105; new Queen met by Alberoni at, 224
Parma, Duke of, 217, 219-20
Peace, negotiations for, commenced, 209; Congress discuss Princess des Ursins' claims, 210-11; Treaty of, concluded, 212
Peterborough, Lord, 88, 93
Philip V., King of Spain (Duke of Anjou), named by Charles II. as his successor, 3; leaves France for Spain, 4; married by proxy to Marie Louise of Savoy, 12; their first meeting, 13-14, 15; refuses to witness auto-da-fé, 24; character of, described by Louis XIV., 25; joins campaign in Italy, 30; approves conduct of Princess des Ursins, 46;

receives letter from Louis XIV., 47; joins campaign in Portugal, 50; thanks Louis XIV. for receiving Princess des Ursins, 69; welcomes her at Canillas, 82-3; besieges Barcelona, 98-9; is defeated and flies, 99-100; obliged to quit Madrid, joins his army, 104; fixes upon Burgos as retreat for the Court, 105; proposes to sell or mortgage crown jewels, 107; change of affairs in favour of, 118-19; joyful return of his troops to Madrid, 121; meets Queen at Segovia, 123; returns to Madrid, 124; letter to Louis XIV. on license of speech, 128; battle of Almanza, 142; advised by Louis XIV. to renounce kingdoms of Spain and the Indies, 175; refuses, 176; promises grandees not to abandon the throne, 178, 185; joins campaign in Aragon, 189; defeated at Saragossa, 196-7; returns to Madrid, is urged again by Louis XIV. to accept terms of Allies, and again refuses to do so, 197-9; second flight from Madrid, establishes Court at Valladolid, 200; returns to Madrid, his joyful reception, visits aged Marquis de Mancera, 204-5; joins army at Guadalaxara, 205; victory of Vallaviciosa, 205-6; his "bed of flags," 206; confers high rank upon Princess des Ursins, 209; peace concluded, firmly established on throne, retains best portions of Spanish dominions, 211; grief at death of wife, 214-15; talks of abdicating, is dissuaded by Princess des Ursins, 215; asks Princess des Ursins to choose a second wife for him, 216; demands the hand of Elizabeth Farnese, 220; is married to her by proxy, 222; consents to her demand for dismissal of Princess des Ursins, 223-4; goes to Guadalaxara, 225-6; letter to Princess des Ursins, 230-1; reinstates Inquisition in full power, 237; sends San Phélipe to visit Princess des Ursins, 239; accords her a pension, 240

Pope, The (Clement IX.), 80; recognises the Archduke as King of Spain, 102; curious attitude of, 139-40, 240

Popoli, Duke de, 105, 109

Port Mahon, loss of, 165

Portocarero, Cardinal, character of, partisan of French interests, 30-1; deals feebly with Admiral of Castile, 38-41; his influence declines, 42; joins party of Archduke, 115; performs Te Deum in his honour, 116; people of Toledo rise against him, 122; pardoned by Philip V., 124; opposes Princess des Ursins' efforts to obtain loan from clergy, 139

Portugal, King of, joins the Grand Alliance, 41

Pretender, is recognised as James III. by Louis XIV., 29; at the Marly balls, 71-2

QUEEN OF SPAIN, Dowager, 82; joins party of the Archduke, 115; people of Toledo rise against her, 122; is escorted out of Spain, 124;

INDEX

Elizabeth Farnese visits her at St. Jean-Pied-de-Port, 224; is close ally of Grand Inquisitor and Alberoni, 224

Queen of Spain. See Elizabeth Farnese

Queen of Spain. See Marie Louise of Savoy

RAMILLIES, battle of, 102

Rénaut, agent of the Duke of Orleans, 183–4; is arrested, 185

Robinèt, Père, 215–16

Rocca, Count I., Prime Minister to Duke of Parma, 217, 220

Rousillon, 100

SALAMANCA, captured by Portuguese, massacre of monks of St. Jerome, 117

San Phélipe, Marquis de (Don Vicente Bacallar), Spanish historian, 84; defends island of Sardinia, 165; evidence against Medina-Cœli, 194–5; visits Princess des Ursins at St. Pierre d'Arène, 239

Santestevan, Comte de, 105

Saragossa, revolt of, 116; battle of, 196–7

Sardinia, island of, lost to Spain, 165

Savoy, Duke of, 4; defection of, 59–60, 173

Segovia, meeting of King and Queen at, 123

Sevigné, Madame de, 7; her letters, 88

Silly, M. de, 144

Spain, condition of, at end of seventeenth century, 16–18; position of women, Oriental customs, 17, 18; Court life, 19–20; peculiar character of warfare in, 119–20

Stanhope, General, urges Archduke to hasten to Madrid, 121; his secret negotiations with the Duke of Orleans, 183–5; tries to win the old Marquis de Mancera to the side of the Archduke, 201–2; forced to lay down arms at Brihuaga, 205

Staremberg, Count, defeated at Villaviciosa, 205–7

St. Jean-de-Luz, reception of Princess des Ursins at, 81; arrival of Princess des Ursins at, 230

St. Jean-Pied-de-Port, new Queen halts at, 224; plot for fall of Princess des Ursins arranged at, 224, 236–7

St. Simon, Duc de, his description of Princess des Ursins, 8–9; his account of her reception in Paris and at Versailles, 65–9; calls upon her, 67–8; with her at Marly, 69–73; his opinion of the Duke of Orleans' plot, 185–6; obtains leave of Duke to visit Princess des Ursins, their interviews, 233–4

St. Simon, Duchesse de, 70–1, 234

Stuarts, Court of, exiled, welcome Princess des Ursins to Rome, 241

Sun, eclipse of, 99

TESSÉ, Marshal, at Canillas, 82, 84-5; besieges Barcelona, 98-9

Toledo, city of, declares for the Archduke, 115; people of, tear down Austrian standard, 122

Torcy, Marquis de, 36, 68, 94, 98, 163; letter from, to Duc de Noailles, 197-9

Toulouse, Count of, blockades harbour of Barcelona, 99

Toulouse, town of, 60, 61, 64

Trimouille, Abbé de la, made Cardinal, 80

URSINS, Princess des (Anne-Marie de la Trimouille), chosen Camarera-Mayor to the Queen-elect of Spain, 5-6; her birth and parentage, 6-7; first and second marriages, 7; is described by St. Simon, 8, 9; friendship with Me. de Maintenon, 9; desires to obtain post of Camarera-Mayor, 10; meets Queen at Villafranca and conducts her into Spain, 12-13; letter written on journey by, 14-15; enlivens Court life at Madrid, 20-1; influence on King and Queen, 24-5; attends sittings of Junta, 30; dares to oppose Inquisition, 33-5; letter on treasure-ships to M. de Torcy, 36-7; urges arrest of Admiral of Castile, 39; her influence increases, 41-2; enmity of the d'Estrées, 43-4; affair of the mutilated despatch, 45-7; her recall determined upon, 47; reprimand from Louis XIV., 48-9; receives order of banishment, 51; chooses her successor, 52; quits Madrid, 54; meets Duc de Grammont at Vittoria, 56; takes up residence at Toulouse, 60; receives permission from Louis XIV. for private audience, 63; commences journey to Paris, 64; is welcomed by Duke of Alva and French Court, 66-7; interviews with Louis XIV., with Duchess of Burgundy, and with Me. de Maintenon, 68; court paid to, 69-71; at the Marly balls, 72-3; "intellectual triumph," 77; urged to return to her post in Spain, 78; "treaty" signed at Marly, 79-80; triumphal journey from Paris to Madrid, 81-5; chooses Amelot as French Ambassador, 86; letter in praise of him, 87; modern style of writing, 88; confers post of Major-domo-Major upon Duke de Frias, 90-2; letter on loss of Barcelona, 93; letter to Torcy urging that troops should be sent from France, 94-7; ditto to Chamillart (same subject), 97-8; letters to Me. de Maintenon on loss of Barcelona and Alcantara, 99-101; on proposed flight of the Queen from Madrid, 102-3; accompanies Queen in flight, 104; letters written during journey 105-10; from Burgos, 110; describes her apartments, 112-13; about poor curé's offering, 114-5; upon loss of Salamanca and massacre of monks of St. Jerome, 117; obtains money to pay troops, 118; describes joyful return of troops and of King and Queen to Madrid, 121-4; letter on dismissal of 300 maids of honour, 126-7; ditto, on calumnious reports, 129-30; free correspondence of, 132-3; letters

INDEX

on character of Philip V., 133; on hope of an heir to the throne, 134-8; writes urging payment to be made to French troops, 138; obtains loan from clergy, 140; letter written before battle of Almanza, 141; ditto, announcing the victory, 143; pictures scene at Marly, 144-5; letter on carnage at Xativa, 146-7; approves of measure to deprive Valencia and Aragon of their privileges, 148-9; her powerful help to Philip's cause, 149; prepares for arrival of infant Prince of Asturias, 150-3; letters on birth of Prince, 153; on infancy of, 154-5; on domestic and social subjects, 156-61; on proposed withdrawal of Berwick, 163-4; on Treaty of Milan, 164; on loss of Port Mahon, 165; on fall of Lille, 167; suspects double dealing on part of Louis XIV., 167-8; tries to prevent his abandoning cause of Philip, 168-9; endeavours to arouse the courage of Me. de Maintenon, 169-71; sends a financial scheme to Versailles, 171-2; inspires Philip with courage to refuse to give up kingdoms of Spain and Indies, 176; causes decree to be issued banishing all Frenchmen from Spain, 179; chooses Duc de Medina-Cœli for leader of new Ministry, 180; urges Chamillart to leave some troops in Spain, 181; letter on Amelot's resignation, 182; discovers treason of Duke of Orleans, 184-5; letters upon Beson's treacherous conduct, 188-90; tries to imbue Me. de Maintenon with hope, 191-2; is nettled at her remarks on female politicians, 193-4; causes the arrest of Medina-Cœli, 194; anger of Orleans faction against, 195-6; position again secure, 196; rejects overtures of Duc de Noailles, 199; again inspires Philip to reject compromise, 199; accompanies Queen to Valladolid, 200; urges Court of Versailles to send Vendôme as Generalissimo to Spain, 202; letter to Vendôme, 202; announces victory of Villaviciosa, 205; success of Philip's cause due to, 207; royal rank conferred upon, 209; desires to possess small principality, 209-11; fails to obtain it, 211; disinterestedness in serving Philip, 211; inaugurates constitutional changes, 211-12; brave contest with Inquisition, 212-14; obtains concessions in favour of English refuges for its victims, 213; prevents Philip's abdication after death of Queen, 214-15; made gouvernante of his children, difficult position, 215; asked by Philip to choose his second wife, 216; induced by Alberoni to advise Philip to marry Elizabeth Farnese, 218-20; appointed Camarera-Mayor to Queen-elect, 221; suspects Alberoni of double dealing, tries to postpone marriage, but fails, 221-2; assists in instituting Academy of Spanish language, 222-3; machinations against her by new Queen, 223-4; goes to Guadraqué to meet Queen, 226; is insulted by her, arrested and sent off under escort of soldiers, 227-8; sufferings on journey to St. Jean-de-Luz, 228-30; receives letter from Philip V., 231; letter to Me. de

Maintenon, 232; arrival at Versailles, 233; conversations with St. Simon, 234; leaves France for Chambéry, 235; receives news of death of Louis XIV., 235-6; objects of her policy in Spain, 236; victim to contest with Inquisition, 236-7; takes up residence at Genoa, and writes from St. Pierre d'Arène, 238-9; visited by San Philèpe and writes to Orry respecting messages brought by him from Philip V., 238-9; takes up residence in Rome, is received with every mark of respect, 240-1; her death, 241; testimonies to her character by St. Simon, Sainte-Beuve, and Geffroy, 241-3

Uzeda, Duc d', 195

VALENCIA, province of, hails Archduke as King of Spain, 93; subjection of, 146; deprived of privileges, 147

Valladolid, Court established at, 200-1, 203

Vaudemont, Prince de, 156, 157

Vendôme, Duc de, commands army in Flanders, 166; is sent as Generalissimo to Spain, 202-3; obliges Archduke to evacuate Madrid, 203; gains battle of Villaviciosa, 205-7; his "bed of flags," 206

Versailles, arrival at, of Princess des Ursins, 67, 233

Vigo, capture of galleons off, by English fleet, 35-8

Villafranca, Marquis de, 90

Villafranca, town of, 12

Villars, Madame de, letters from, 18, 24

Villaviciosa, battle of, 205-7

Villeroy, Duc de (Marshal), is defeated at Ramillies, 102, 171, 232, 235

Vittoria, 59, 81, 205

WILLIAM III., 29-30, 121

War of Spanish Succession commences, 30; in many respects a religious war, 139-40; draws to a close, 208

XATIVA, carnage at, 146

Printed by BALLANTYNE, HANSON & Co.
London & Edinburgh

www.ingramcontent.com/pod-product-compliance
Lightning Source LLC
Chambersburg PA
CBHW032047230426
43672CB00009B/1505